From Depression to Deliverance

How God can heal your heart in 30 days!

By: Taquila Coleman

**Printed in the United States of America**

CreateSpace Independent Publishing Platform

First Printing, 2017

**ISBN-13: 978-1545166338**

**ISBN-10: 1545166331**

**Ordering Information:**

Quantity Sales. Special discounts are available on quantity purchases by corporations, associations, and others. For details, contact Taquila Coleman by visiting www.TaquilaColeman.com.

## ACKNOWLEDGMENTS

To God be the Glory. All praise goes to God for delivering me from depression and birthing my calling through the process.

A special thank you to my book coach, Kim Brooks, who has believed in me, pushed me beyond my limit, and helped me throughout this process. I truly appreciate you!

Thank you to Angela Maritim, my Therapist, for allowing God to use you to comfort and encourage me in our sessions. You were the first person to hear about my book, which was inspired by God. Thanks for all of your help!

To my three blessings, Da'Jour, Jaylen, and Miracle; dreams do come true, and mommy loves you.

Thank you to all the family members and friends who have stayed up many nights listening to me talk about my book; I appreciate each and every one of you.

**Table of Contents**

Scriptures on Love

Scriptures on Healing

Scriptures on Identity

# Introduction

*From depression to deliverance* is written from the standpoint of a single mom suffering from depression because of the broken relationships in my life. Being a single mom is hard work, and it is even more difficult when the father of your child is refusing to help you or be a part of his child's life. It is my intention to inspire hope within every single mom raising children on their own, battling depression, feeling all alone in this cold world—knowing that just how God delivered me from depression, He will do the same thing for you.

How to read this book: Part one of this book talks about the people and situations in my life that contributed to my depression and how it all led me to counseling for help. Part two takes you on my journey of healing the wounds inside of me. It shows you exactly what I did and what you must do in order to bring healing into your life. Part three is the revelation that God gave to me on why from time to time, after doing all of the inner work, I still would feel depressed. God revealed to me that deliverance was much needed in my life, and I will show you exactly how to do it in your own life so that you are set free from the spirit of depression. In part four, you will read about the development that God took me through after going through this process. There are some things that God wants to show and develop within you, to help you win in this thing called life.

At the end of the day, all you need is hope and strength. Hope that it will get better and strength to hold on until it does.

# Chapter 1: He wants an abortion, but I don't

Who would have thought saying those two words would negatively impact my life and send me into a deep depression? I sat, holding the phone up to my ear, wondering to myself, *How am I going to tell this man that I'm pregnant? I mean, how is he going to act or respond to the news?* As I sat there, deep in my thoughts, I heard him say, "Taquila, what's wrong? Just tell me; you can talk to me." Before I knew it, the words "I'm pregnant" was escaping from my lips and I heard nothing but silence on the other end of the telephone. After a minute had passed, he finally spoke, "I can't have any more kids. I'm going to be 44-years-old this year." After hearing his words, anger overtook me, and I said, "Well, you should have thought of that before having sex!" "Look, I'm not trying to argue with you. I don't want any more kids. I have to get my life together; me together. This world is messed up," he said. He went on and on, trying to convince me why he didn't want children anymore, but the truth of the matter was that I was pregnant. "I heard everything you said, but at the end of the day, I'm pregnant with your child. So what are you going to do about it?" Then he spoke the words I will never forget, "Why don't you have a baby by someone who wants a baby by you?" On hearing those words, it felt like someone punched me in the chest and all the wind left my body. *How could this man who told me he loved me, asked me if I was his wife, say such thing? I thought you loved me, cared for me ...* As I sat there, crying, I said to him, "I was wrong about you," and hung up the phone. I never heard from him again after that phone call.

From that moment on, I was determined to raise my son on my own with or without his father. Somewhere deep in my heart, I wanted to believe that my son's father would change his mind and desire to be in his son's life, but each time I called him, his phone would go straight to voice mail, and if I sent a text message, he never responded back, so I guess I was on my own. I remember, at 24 weeks pregnant with my son, I was playing outside with my oldest son, trying to show him how to ride his bike without training wheels on. I would jog behind him as he was learning how to ride his bike. Later on, that night, as I got out of the shower, I felt extra water running down my legs, so I immediately sat down on the toilet and then came a gush of blood. *OMG! What is going on? Am I having a miscarriage?* All these thoughts rushed through my mind as I picked up my cell phone to call my mother and tell her what was going on with me. She asked me to hang up the phone and call 911 because it sounded like

I was having a miscarriage and that she was on her way back to the house because my car at the time was down and waiting on the EMS at that time in my life was not an option. As I called 911 and told them what was going on, the operator advised me to get off the toilet and to unlock all the doors so the EMS could get into my unit. As I hung up the phone, I told my older son to get dressed because we're leaving. As I was leaving out of the house, my uncle pulled up and asked me to get into the truck, and he took me up the street to the nearest hospital where I was at for the next two months. After the doctors had checked me, they advised me that I did not have a miscarriage, but my water did break at 24 weeks and that I had to stay in the hospital on bed rest until I had my baby. In my mind, I thought I was going to deliver my baby within the next couple of hours since my water had broken, but the doctors gave me medicine to stop the labor and told me it was too early for me to deliver my baby. His lungs weren't fully developed, so with that, they advised me to be on bed rest in the hospital, and that they were going to try their possible best to keep my baby inside of me as long as possible.

I always thought once your water breaks, then next is the baby, but not in my situation. Each day as I stayed in the hospital, I constantly drank cups of water. The doctors stated that the point where my water broke at the hole would seal up on its own as long as I stayed in bed and continued to drink water. I was able to keep my baby inside of me until I delivered at 30 weeks. Spending those two months in the hospital drove me crazy mentally. I couldn't do anything but lie in bed, watch TV, eat, and drink water. In the hospital, I ended up getting into it with my father over a misunderstanding, and I remember sitting there, thinking all the men in my life had turned their back on me. At that time in my life, my relationship with my brother was not good, I just got into it with my father, and the father of my unborn child does not want anything to do with his child or me. Each night as I laid in bed in the hospital, I would cry, get mad, angry, and allow bitterness to set within me over my situation.

Once home, I really fell into a depressed state because my car was down, which meant I couldn't go anywhere—just sit in the house and look at the walls and TV again. I started to feel like I was losing my mind each day that I sat in the house. It didn't make it any better having a newborn son home with me because all he did was cry every hour on the hour, which also drove me crazy. I really wished that people would come to my house to see me, just sit and talk with me or come over to help me out sometimes and give me a break. However, the only person I saw was my cousin who would stop by here and there and give the baby a bath for me while I take a quick nap and shower.

Things started looking up for me when my son turned 6 months old. I finally started sorting things out in my mind regarding my son's father, and I finally stopped blaming myself for the reason why he didn't want to be in his son's life. At that time, I started talking to a friend of mine who was married but living in a different house from his wife. I met him at church in one of the classes I took there. He ended up being my accountability partner, and ever since, we stayed in contact with each another. I never liked him more than a friend because I thought that he was cold-hearted and mean, plus, he was still married. He would call and check on me after I had my son; he knew what I was going through, with my son's father not wanting to be in my son's life. Acting just like a friend, he would listen to me, allow me to vent off my anger and frustration and just be there for me the best way he knew how.

My friend and I started talking every day, all day, and I started looking at him as more than a friend, and I sensed the same thing from him, so we began to take our friendship to another level—the sex level. You know what the sex level is, right? That's the level when two friends get together and start having sex with one another without any commitment. Yes, friends with benefits, whatever you want to call it. I'd kept telling myself, *I am not going to fall for him; we're just friends having sex here and there,* but the truth of the matter was that each day that I sat on the phone talking to him for hours at a time, I was falling for him. I mean, he called me when he woke up in the morning, when he arrived at work, on his break, when he got home from work and right before he went to bed at night. Who wouldn't fall for someone giving you that kind of attention on a daily basis, and on top of all, the talking throughout the day? He also was helping my older son with baseball and homework. Everything seemed fine between him and I, and my son liked him too, but everything changed the day I called him at work and told him I was Pregnant! "No, no, no! I'm done having kids. You have to get an abortion. I will pay for it, but I can't have any more kids." *Here we go again,* I thought to myself. One year later and this is happening to me again. "I don't believe in having an abortion" was what I told him. "OK, what about giving the baby up for adoption?" What? No, he didn't just tell me to give my baby up for an adoption. After that, I simply told him that I would call him back and hung up the phone. As I sat there in shock and disbelief, I just couldn't

14

believe that this was happening to me all over again. I guess if I had learned my lesson the first time, I wouldn't be in this situation again.

I was so stressed out and didn't know what to do, who to turn to for help because I felt like a fool getting pregnant again almost a year and a half later by a man that don't want me to have his baby and is married. I thought if I gave him time to think about everything and sort things out in his mind that he would change his mind and come around, but boy, I was wrong. Each time that he called me, we started arguing because he was adamant about me having an abortion or giving my baby up for adoption. One day, he called me over to his house to talk face-to-face about everything, and as he started talking, he reminded me of how jacked up my life already was and couldn't see any reason to bring a baby into my already jacked up life. He reminded me that if it weren't for my mother, I would be living out on the streets somewhere. And to add insult to injury, he gave me $50 supposedly for my belated birthday that he just so happened miss. In my mind, when he gave me the money, I thought to myself, *Does he think giving me $50 is going to get rid of me?* Whatever the case was to him, I took the $50 and put it in my pocket as an early child support gift to his unborn child and let him think whatever he liked. After allowing him to go on and on about my jacked up life, I got up and told him, "I have to go to work; talk to you later," and left. After leaving his house and replaying all the negative words he spoke to me, I started pondering the thought of having an abortion ... *I mean, he doesn't want to be in the baby's life, and he's right; I am struggling, so why have another baby by a man that doesn't want one by me?* My decision and mind was made up. *I'm having an abortion, and I'm going to be done with him, end of story.* At that thought, I picked up my cell phone and called my friend up to tell her about my new decision.

As I sat there on the phone talking with my friend and telling her that I was going to have the abortion because I didn't want to raise another child on my own all by myself and that I was tired of struggling, she sat on the other end listening to me go on and on and when I was done, she said, "Well, you know, I'm against abortion, and you're going to struggle anyway it goes, so you might as well have your baby. Will it be easy? No, but you will be OK, and if he doesn't want to be in his child's life, then that is his loss," and after that, she started praying for me right there on the phone.

# The Abortion Clinic

My mind was made up; *I am having an abortion.* He was happy about my decision. I was 12 weeks pregnant, so I called and made myself an appointment and told him how much it was going to cost him and to have the money ready the day of my appointment. The night before my appointment, I couldn't sleep, my spirit was not at ease, so I decided to pray. I just wanted the pressure off me and for everything to return to normal, and I go on about my business and vice versa. In my prayer, I simply talked to God and told Him what was on my mind and how I was feeling. I told God, "I really didn't want to have an abortion, but I'm under so much pressure right now that I really didn't know what to do." I asked God to forgive me ahead of time for what I was going to do the next day and to give me the strength to get through it.

As I woke up the next day, getting myself ready to have this procedure done, I couldn't help but notice that I wasn't feeling stressed out or anxious, but at peace. I thought that was strange but didn't think anything of it, just thought to myself, *God heard my prayers, and He has me at peace about what I'm about to do.* My ex arrived to pick me up on time as scheduled, and off we headed to the abortion clinic. As we entered the clinic, I couldn't believe how many women were inside, waiting to be seen. I immediately scanned the room for a familiar face and saw none, so I was relieved because I didn't want anyone to know that I was about to have an abortion. The lady behind the desk handed me some paperwork to fill out and when I was done, to give it back to her along with the fee for the services. After I filled out everything and handed her all my paperwork along with the money, I sat back down next to him. We began to talk like we once did before I got pregnant. For the first time since I got pregnant, we were actually getting along, not arguing with one another.

As I sat, waiting for them to call my name, I couldn't help but observe the faces of the ladies and how they looked when each of them came from the back—having had the procedure done. They each had the same look on their face; it was like a blank stare, like a different spirit came over them. Their eyes looked cold but sad at the same time. I started to wonder, *Will I have this same look in my eyes?*

"Taquila Coleman ..." *They're calling my name to go to the back.* As I got up and started walking to the back, the lady placed me in a room to go in and told me to get undressed so that they can check me on the ultrasound to see how far along I was. As I undressed and got up onto the table and laid down, I noticed that I was still at peace, not scared of anything. In walked this lady who began to pour gel onto my belly and see how far along I was on the ultrasound. The lady checked and looked at the ultrasound twice and then said, "Wait right here; you have to see the doctor." After about five minutes of waiting, in walked the doctor, who was a man, and he looked at the ultrasound and then looked again and then said to me, "Are you sure you want to do this?" *Huh? What? Why did you say that?* "Because you are 17 weeks pregnant, not 12 weeks, and if you are going to go forward with this, then this will be a two-day procedure, so we will start some of the procedures today, and you will have to come back tomorrow to finish the rest." I asked him, "How much does it cost?" He continued to stare at the monitor and had a confused look on his face, and he blurted out $5,000. Soon as I heard him say that to me, I got up off the table and told him no, that I was not having an abortion, and started putting my clothes back on. He told me, after I got dressed, to go and wait out in the other waiting room for my discharge papers and my money back. As I sat down in the waiting room in the back, another lady was sitting there, crying right in front of me. I felt so sorry for her. I didn't know if she had had the abortion already or if she was conflicted with her decision. She got up and went into the restroom and continued to cry some more. My heart was so heavy for that young lady. I kept wondering to myself, *God, why are You showing me all of this?* I didn't know why then, but now, I know why God allowed me to go through all of that.

Women are being pressured all of the time to have an abortion by their boyfriend, and the pressure and him threatening to leave if you do not abort is what causes most women to abort their unborn child and later regret it. This needs to stop. Somebody has to be the voice for our women, and I choose to be that voice for you. Listen, never allow anyone to talk you into doing something that you don't want to do. If you do not believe in abortion, then don't do it, period! If he continues to threaten to leave you, then show him the door. God is showing you his true color and how he acts and handles situation under pressure. You don't need any boy like this in your life. Let him go so that God can make a man out of him and teach him how to take care of his responsibility. Children are a blessing from the Lord (Psalm 127:3.) If God has blessed you with the ability to have a child, then do not abort; who's to say that God will allow for you to have another baby later on down the line? You don't know, and it's not worth it.

If you are currently pregnant and your boyfriend is pressuring you to have an abortion, but you don't know what to do, then my advice to you is to do nothing. Do not make an emotional decision while under pressure that you will later regret. Ask your baby daddy to give you enough space to think clearly so that you can make your own decision. If he continues to tell you that he is not going to be in the child's life, then believe him and let him go. You are better off without him. I know you're thinking, *But what about my child? I want my child's father to be in his or her life.* And I agree, but your child's father is telling you where he stands with you and the baby; you must believe him and decide to raise your baby on your own. We all want our children's father to be present in their life, but it has to be his choice and right now, he is refusing to be there for his child, so he has to go. One thing that I know about God is that if you take care of the children that He bless you with and do well with them, then God will take care of you and your baby. Now, will there be some struggle here and there? Absolutely, but that is part of life, learning and growing, but the Bible says that God will never leave you nor forsake you; He is always by your side. Choose life and trust God!

## Chapter 2: Everything was fine until I got pregnant

*How did I end up here? I mean, everything seemed to be going good until I got pregnant.* I really believed that if I didn't get pregnant, he would have divorced his wife and asked me to marry him. *Maybe it's me! I shouldn't have said the things that I said to him over the phone; it probably hurt his feelings. I should have been more understanding with him and listened to what he was saying when he expressed his concerns about not wanting to have another child. I really miss him; maybe I should call him and tell him how I feel. You know what? Forget him; I'm not contacting him. If he doesn't want to be with me anymore, then it's his loss, not mine. I'm going to raise my baby on my own with or without him.*

Almost every day, I found myself thinking thoughts such as the ones above. I was starting to believe that I was going crazy and losing my mind. I tried my best to stop thinking about my daughter's father. I tried keeping myself busy with the kids and housework, but nothing seemed to help. I had another friend who would call me and talk to me here and there, but I told him I did not want to jump into anything until I was fully over my child's father. He seemed understanding and continued to call me up until he passed away. Now, I have to deal with him passing away and my daughter's father acting a fool. I knew in my heart that I deserved better; it was these feelings that wouldn't go away and the constant thoughts about him, how he made me laugh and feel special. *Lord, I just want to move on with my life and forget all about him.*

# Child Support

*Today is the day that I will see my daughter's father for the
first time after having my baby. I wonder how he will act.
Will he say hi to me or ignore me and act like I don't exist?*
All these crazy thoughts kept running through my mind as I
made my way down to the friend of the court building. I got
there a little early so that I can get a good seat that positions
me to see if and when he walked through that door. I thought
he was going to have his daughter bring him down there
since he's legally blind and unable to drive, but boy was I
wrong when I saw him walk in there with another woman.
Before seeing that other woman, I thought I was over him but
the fire I felt inside of me as I looked at this woman walking
in with my daughter's father let me know that I wasn't over
him and had more work to do within myself. After several
minutes had passed, I was able to calm myself down by
convincing myself that he only came down here with this
woman to piss me off and see me act a fool in this court;
therefore, I didn't. I didn't say one word to him or her; kept
my head looking straight at the TV in front of me like he
didn't exist. After 30 minutes or so, they finally called us into
the back to see the judge concerning our case. Once back
there, I wasn't expecting for him to tell the judge that he did
not want any parenting time with his child. If looks could

kill, he would have been up in heaven, talking to God that day. The judge looked surprised that he said that and then looked over at me and asked me if I was fine with his response and I said that's fine. There were other things that were said and done by him in court, but through it all, I kept my composure even though I was hurting inside. Once home, everyone wanted to know how it went, if he showed up, and what the things he said were. I told them what happened and how I had left the court, feeling like a fool. *How could I possibly love someone cold hearted like that? What did I do to deserve this?* I wrapped my arms around my daughter and told her I love her even if daddy don't.

# Chapter 3: No One Likes Me!

Do you ever feel like the people in your life are just tolerating you and don't really like you? I mean, whenever they have a problem and need to talk to someone, you're always there for them to talk to and give them advice regarding their problems, but when you need someone to talk to, they act like they don't want to hear it or like you're getting on their nerves and don't want to be bothered. Yes, this is exactly what I was surrounded by—people who really didn't like me but tolerated me.

Tony Gaskin posted a quote that read, "They Don't hate you; they hate themselves and take it out on you." I lived in an apartment complex that consists of my mother, brother, and cousin living in the same building. This cousin who lived over there was someone whom I consider to be one of my favorite cousin on my dad's side of the family. Her mother, my auntie, was my favorite auntie on my dad's side because she was the only one out of all my dad's sisters that would take time out to come and get me as a child and spend time with me, so I loved her for that. Her daughter and I constantly bumped heads with one another as we got older, and for the life of me, I couldn't figure out why our relationship was always shaky until she moved into the same building I was living in. My cousin would have parties at her house and would invite everyone in the family over except me. I would go over to my cousin's unit to see about her and sometimes sit and talk with her but not once did she visit me at my place and we stayed in the same apartment complex. My brother stayed down the hall from me, and he tried so hard to hide his true feeling towards me. My mother raised my brother and I not to be close with one another; she played favoritism between the two of us and planted lies in his heads about me, which has affected our relationship until this day. My mother is someone whom I have labeled to be narcissistic; everything is all about her and her world. My mother played a big part with me suffering from depression because of the many games she played in my life. One minute she would act like she liked me, come up to my unit and see my kids and me, and then the next minute when the other personality would kick in, she would act as though she didn't want to be bothered by me, like she didn't like me and could care less about me. I made the decision that I was going to stay to myself and not bother anyone because everyone seemed so unstable and acted like they didn't like me, but the minute I stopped all the phone calls and wasn't going up to their unit, then here they came calling me:

"What's wrong with you? I haven't heard from you; are you OK?" Don't you hate it when people act like they don't know why you stopped calling them? Each time, I would fall into their trap and start back calling them and going over to their house only for them to do the same thing to me, all over again.

I continued to hang around them and tried to overlook how they were treating me, but each time, it just drove me into a deep depression. I started believing that I was a bad person; they constantly called me mean, so I believed that about myself and thought maybe that was why they didn't want to be around me. The devil is a liar. Maya Angelou said, "When people show you who they are, believe them." My family was showing me exactly who they were and how they felt about me; I just wasn't listening. One day as I was talking to my cousin, I stated to her how I just couldn't understand why I kept getting into it with certain females, and she said, "They see something in you that they don't see in themselves," and at that moment, a lightbulb went off inside my head. My cousin just told me what the problem was between her and I and the problem that I was also having with other family members and friends. They saw something in me that they wished they possessed. There's a quote that says, "Don't let someone dim your light simply because it's shining in their eyes." I always felt like I had to play small and shrink myself back to fit in with the crowd in order for them to like me but I was starting to get tired of dumbing myself down just so the next person can feel OK with themselves. I was beginning to sense in my spirit that God was calling me to something greater in life with or without my family.

## Chapter 4: I'm Exhausted & Need a Break!

Every day is the same old routine; wake up, take my son to school, come home to tend to my two other children, cook breakfast, lunch and dinner, clean up, do the laundry, pick my son up from school, go to the grocery store, back home, help my son with homework, give the kids a bath and off to bed ... I'm exhausted and don't have time for me. Each day, it's the same thing, looking at the same white walls, always in the house, never get to go out and have fun or do anything for myself. When I want to get my hair done, the kids are right there with me. When I want to go and see a movie, I have to take the kids with me, and nine times out of ten, I'm missing the movie because my two-year-old don't want to sit down but wants to walk around the movie theater and see what's going on, so I stopped going to the movies. My kids and I go out to eat at different restaurants, but again, I can't enjoy myself because if I'm not screaming and yelling at my son, I'm chasing him around the restaurant, trying to get him to sit down quietly.

Being a single mom is hard work. I don't think people understand exactly what we go through. I have three children, so once I tend to one and get him settled, I have to move on to the next one and get him together and then make sure my daughter is alright as well. By the time I get to me, I'm exhausted and just want to go to sleep. I know you're probably wondering, *Well, how about you put your children in daycare to give yourself a break from time to time?* Well, let's talk about daycare and how I quit my job to stay at home to watch my own kids.

April of 2016, I received a job offer from one of the big automotive companies to work in their plant making good money. I was excited and thought to myself, *This is the break that I've been waiting for; this job is going to help provide for my family and move us away from our current environment.* Once I started working at this new job, one thing that I noticed right off the back was that daycare is expensive when you have three children. I ended up hiring a nanny to watch my children while I was at work and also to take and pick up my oldest son from school for me. The nanny only lasted for a week because of her fees, so I found an in-home daycare that was 30 minutes away from my house to put my children in while I worked. Everything seemed to be going fine and working itself out until after the third day—I was advised that my children cannot come back to daycare because of the crying and its effect on the other children. In two and a half weeks, I spent close to $1000 on childcare and was drained and frustrated with everyone. I turned to the state for help with assistance, but they only paid $15 for two of my children. *Why does being a single mom have to be so hard?* I was not liking this life!

## No Help from Family

I have always been the type that would go out of my way to help anyone in need, but now that I need help with my children, no one is there for me. In one year, I have had three good jobs but unable to keep them because of not being able to afford daycare for my three children. Every time I ask my family to watch my children for me while I go to work, the answer was always no, or they would give me some excuse as to why they can't help me. My mom would offer to watch her grandchildren, but because she really doesn't want to do it, we always seem to get into it over my children, and she ends up quitting on me right in the middle of me being at work. I got to the point where I just accepted the fact that for whatever reason, my family chose not to help me with my children, but yet they watch everyone else's children. I felt like the people I loved the most turned their back on me when I needed them the most. This caused me to fall into a deep depression because no one likes to think that their own family doesn't like them. The pain was too much for me to take because I didn't understand why they were acting this way. My way of dealing with the pain was by isolating myself in the house from everyone and leaving my family alone. Once inside the house, I turned to food for comfort and would eat, eat, and eat. I ate so much food that I gained an extra 15 pounds by just sitting in the house, watching TV, eating sweets, and drinking pop all day. It wasn't long before my depression started to show on the outside. There were days when my neighbor would come up to my unit and knock on my door, wanting my son to come out and play with her son and I would answer the door with my hair sticking straight up all over my head. I didn't care how I looked backed then, so I always wore big jogging pants and a t-shirt. One day, my neighbor said to me while standing at my door, looking at me, "If you ever want me to watch the kids for you while you take a quick shower or take a nap, I'm right upstairs." I appreciated her offering to watch my children for me, but at that moment, I thought to myself, *Dang! I must really look like I need a shower or a nap.* That day on, I tried my best to get up each day and take care of myself, but it was a struggle.

# Chapter 5: The Narcissistic Mother

As I sit here thinking to myself on why I don't have any friends, the thought comes to mind that just maybe the reason why I don't have any friends and can't seem to get along with other women is because of my own relationship with my mother. I'm starting to believe that there may be some truth to this ...

My mom and I always had a shaky relationship. We could never seem to get along, and for the life of me, I couldn't figure out why. My brother and my mom, on the other hand, had a perfect relationship in my eyes. Whenever he needed help, she was always there for him. When he needed a babysitter, she watched his children. My mom gave me the same treatment but with conditions ... "I will help you if you do as I say"; "I will watch your kids if you pay me." I found out early on that if I made my mother upset or mad for any reason that she would later get back at me and refuse to help me. In my eyes, my mother liked to see me struggle and I couldn't figure out why. I always felt like my mother treated me like some chick off the street that was one of her enemies. A couple of my family members told me that my mom was jealous of me, but it's hard to believe that your own mother could be jealous of you. I knew some of the problems I was having with my mom was because of how her mom treated her growing up as a child. She did not have the mother-daughter type of relationship with her mother, so I guess this is why she and I don't have that type of relationship too.

I stumbled upon the book *Will I Ever Be Good Enough?: Healing the Daughters of Narcissistic Mothers* by Dr. Karyl McBride Ph.D. and boy was I glad to have found and read that book. After reading the book, I discovered that my mother was narcissistic and that one of the reasons why she and I can't seem to get along is because when my mother looks at me, she doesn't see her daughter, but she sees herself. Also, when she looks at her son, my brother, she sees her son, which is why she treats us different.


Even though my depression started back when I was a teenager, I didn't begin to notice it until I moved closer to my mom. We stayed in the same apartment complex, and the purpose of me moving closer to her was so that I could get help with my children, but it seemed like that was one of the worst things that I could have ever done. My mom was the head person over the complex, which meant she had the authority to put whomever she didn't like or want there out on the streets. Since I could never keep a job because of car being down or not having a reliable babysitter, I was always behind in my rent. Whenever I didn't do as she said, she would threaten to put my children and I out on the streets. I was always worried about the day my mom was going to evict my kids and me. I had no doubt in my mind that she would put me out because she did it before in the past. This is what kept me feeling depressed because I felt hopeless in my situation. I knew I couldn't work because I couldn't afford daycare and I was a year behind in my rent, so I couldn't figure out how I was going to get caught up in my rent before my mother put us out. So to keep my mother happy, I gave her whatever she wanted, even if it meant taking from my household to give to her. She knew what she was doing and enjoyed every minute of it. I was receiving food stamps back then, and I was getting enough just to feed my three children and I, and instead of my mother looking at it as a way to feed my children, she saw it as a benefit to her. Therefore, she would ask me to buy her food with them, and I did until one day I discovered that she had me buying food for someone else in the family; that's when I said enough is enough and cut her off.

Each time that I got a job, my mother would volunteer to watch my kids for me and then later do things to try and get me fired from work and so I stopped trusting her and just stayed at home, watching my own children. I kept telling myself, when I have the opportunity to get away from her, I'm taking it because I noticed that my mother was jealous of me and didn't have my best interest at heart. Also, the type of relationship I had with my mother was one of the reasons why I was having problems connecting with other women.

I share my story with you about my mother because I meet many women who have mother wounds and are afraid to talk about it. They hold it in and think they are the reason why they can't get along with their mother, but that's not always the case. Even though my mother has traits of a narcissistic, I also know that my grandmother treated my mother the exact same way she treated me. My mother is repeating what her mother did to her to me. Is it right? Not at all, but I understand why my mom and I do not have the mother and daughter type of relationship that I always wanted to have with her. God also showed me what I was really fighting against that's disguising itself as my mother. The spirit of rejection, the spirit of sexual perversion that I would narrow down to being an abused as a child, the spirit of bitterness, and other things. The Bible says, "For our struggle is not against flesh and blood, but against the rulers, against the authorities, against the powers of this dark world and against the spiritual forces of evil in the heavenly realms" (Ephesians 6:12 NIV). My problem is not with my mother, but with the demonic spirits that are within her; that's what I'm fighting against. You have to become aware of the tactic that the devil is using that causes you to stay into it with your mother. You're not fighting her but the spirit. This is a spiritual battle that must be fought in the spiritual realm.

My advice to you who are having a hard time getting along with your mother is to pray first and ask God to show you the problem at hand. Secondly, if you have not dealt with the issues you have concerning your mother, then I suggest you go and seek a counselor so that he/she can help you get to the root of the problem and help you heal from the mother wounds you have residing within you. Third, turn to God to make you whole again. There is only so much that a therapist can do, a pastor can do, and you can do in your own life; sometimes, you have to talk to God and allow Him to heal and restore you back to wholeness. Lastly, you have to separate yourself from your mother so that God can do the necessary work that He needs to do within you. God has to heal certain wounds in you and teach you how to set healthy boundaries with your mother so that you are dealing with her in a healthy manner.

# Chapter 6: I Need Help!

Have you ever felt like something was wrong with you? Like something was just not right with you, but you just couldn't put your finger on it, yet you knew inside something wasn't right? That's exactly how I was feeling the day I decided to call and schedule me an appointment for counseling. I knew something was off within me because one minute I would be feeling great, happy about life, making plans on doing this and that and then the next minute, I would feel sad and have no desire to do anything but lay around in my bed and sleep all day. There were days when I would wake up and don't feel like taking a shower or doing my hair. Sometimes, I would leave out of the house, looking any kind of way, because I didn't care about how I looked or who saw me. I always felt tired with no energy. For the life of me, I couldn't make a decision on what I wanted to do regarding my life because I was always changing my mind. I lived in a state of confusion; confused about this, confused if he still liked me or not, confused about my purpose. When my friends would call me up and invite me out somewhere, sometimes, I would go if I could take my kids with me, such as the park, but once there, I was ready to go back home and sit in the house.

There were times when I just didn't have a desire for life. I really wanted to change my life, but what I was doing was not changing anything. I remember the first time the thought of seeing someone for depression came to mind and just like that; I talked myself out of it by telling myself, *There is nothing wrong with you, I will feel better tomorrow. I just need to take a nap,* and sometimes I did feel better the next day, but a week later, I'm back sitting in the house, crying over I don't know what, mad, upset with everyone, hating my life, and yelling and cursing at my kids. It was time to get some help ...

I went online and searched in Google *counseling services in Detroit* to see what listing would come up. As I searched and viewed different websites, there was one website that stood out to me. Under the service tab, she had a couple of key words that caught my attention such as parenting support, therapy for depression, women and self-esteem issues, and anger management. These words spoke to me because my 2-year-old was out of control; I knew that I was depressed from doing my own research online. I was always angry and mad about something, so I knew I had some anger issues inside of me and because I didn't feel good about myself and at that time couldn't get along with other women and the repeated pattern of bad relationships with men, I knew somewhere inside of me I had some self-esteem issues going on. I just didn't know where and how to find the underlying cause of them. I called and scheduled an appointment, and immediately after making my appointment, my mind started racing about who is going to watch my kids while I go to counseling and how I was wasting my time, I'm going to be in counseling for a long time because of all of my issues, and all these other thoughts. I yelled and said, "ENOUGH! I'm going to counseling. My momma is going to watch these kids, and I'm going to get the help that I need. I'm tired of this." And just like that, my mind was made up, and all the thoughts left my mind.

The day of my first session, I woke up excited and ready to go. I got my kids ready to go to grandma's house and told her I had a doctor's appointment to go to, that the kids couldn't come along, therefore, dropped the kids off with her early that morning. I was ready to get down to the bottom of things. I was sick and tired of being sick and tired of my life. When I arrived, I was handed some forms to fill out, and I was also given several questions to answer to see where I was on the scale with depression and anxiety. After answering all of the questions and calculating up all of my scores for each section, I found that I had severe depression, severe anxiety, and post-partum depression. WOW! I didn't know my depression was severe like that; maybe that's why I always felt like I was on the edge, ready to go off any second. I was escorted to the back in a room where our sessions will be held at, and once inside, it was very cozy, I have to say. There was soft gospel music playing in the background, quotes of scriptures were on the walls in picture formats, and then my session started. She started with questions about myself, the reason why I came in today and what I was expecting to get out of our counseling session with each other. I remember as I started talking and sharing with her some of the things that were going on in my life, I started to tear up inside. I got quiet for a second and started listening to the words of the gospel song that was playing in the background and I started crying. It felt like the Lord was comforting me right there in that moment with His words from the song. It makes me think about what God's words say: "Praise be to the God and Father of our Lord Jesus Christ, the Father of compassion and the God of all comfort, [4] who comforts us in all our troubles, so that we can comfort those in any trouble with the comfort we ourselves receive from God" (2 Corinthians 1:3-4). We never know how God is going to show up in our lives. Who would have ever thought my process of healing started with hearing the lyrics from a gospel song. I knew in that moment that I was in the right place and that my season of depression, feeling unloved and unwanted was about to come to an end because I decided to do something about my life. I decided to stop the emotional roller coaster, the ups and down, the playing the victim role and feeling sorry for myself. I knew in my heart my life was about to change and turn around for the better right there in that room in those sessions; all I had to do was show up and do the work.

# Part 2: The Solution: Inner Healing

# Chapter 7: Let Him Go!

January of 2016 was a dark time in my life. I already had my daughter and my daughter's father was keeping his word of not being in my daughter's life. Eight months has passed since having my daughter, and her father hasn't come to see her. He calls on the phone and asks about her here and there, but no effort is being made on his end of seeing her or being in her life. I was at the point in time of my life where I was tired of being nice to him, tired of wondering if he will ever come around; I wanted to just cut him off completely and never tell my daughter about him. Before I made any foolish decision that I may later regret, I decided to fast and seek God's face concerning the matter, and so I did. I fasted for five days straight, first time ever fasting in my life, so I wasn't sure if I was doing it right, but I had faith that God heard my prayers and was going to answer my prayers in due time. In my prayer, I specifically asked God what I was supposed to do with him. *Is he the one I'm going to later marry? Can I just cut him off and go on like he never exists?* All of these questions I asked God, believing that He heard me and was going to answer my prayer. Two weeks after fasting, I forgot all about my prayers to God and wasn't paying attention when God gave me my first dream with my daughter's father in it and I was letting him go. I woke up from that dream, thinking why I was dreaming about him. Not thinking much about it, just wanting to get over him and move on with my life and make him a distance memory in my past. Each time that I ask God to reveal something to me, I also ask that He gives me a double confirmation of His answer so that just in case I missed it the first time, I won't miss it the second. The next night, God gave me a second dream similar to the first dream with my daughter's father in it, and in this dream, he was sitting down in a chair away from me, smiling at me and I was kneeling down by a bookshelf looking at him, thinking, *I got to let him go.* Each time that I had that thought, he just kept looking at me with a smile on his face, and then I woke up and it hit me. God is telling me to let him go!

God was very clear and straight forward with me in both of my dreams, and the message in the dream was, "Let him go." *However, is he the man I'm supposed to marry?* "I said let him go!" *What am I supposed to do about him?* "Let him go!" *What do I tell my daughter about him?* "Let him go!" It is funny how when we ask God to reveal something to us, and He does, and we do not like the answer, we begin to question Him and wonder if we really heard God correctly.

God is very direct with His answers, and God also knew that I could be a little hard headed too, so that following Sunday while at church, He had my pastor preach a sermon on "letting go." Sitting in church, listening to my pastor preach directly to me about letting people go from my life and how if you continue to hold on to the people who God wants you to let go of, He will allow for them to continue to reject and hurt you until you let them go. I knew the message was for me and so that day, I let him go.

Here is a couple of reasons why God wanted me to let him go:

1. I've made my daughter's father an idol in my life. Whenever I had a problem, I went to him and sought his advice, against going to God in prayer and seeking His guidance concerning the things in my life.

2. He's still married, and God is not going to give me another woman's husband. In my fasting, I ask God to reveal to me if he was still married or not so that I could know how to proceed with him, but the truth of the matter is, I had no business crossing the line, sleeping with another woman's husband, even if they stay in different houses. On paper and in God's eyesight, they are still married.

3. God wants me to let him go and focus on building my relationship with Him.

4. God could not work in my life as long as my mind and heart was on my daughter's father.

5. God wanted me to get my house in order and in right standing with Him.

6. God has someone better in store for me, but in order for me to receive what God has for me, I have to let go of what's blocking my blessing and allow God to heal me inside so that when the time is right, I will receive what my heart truly desire.

And with those thoughts in mind, I let go and allowed God to begin to work in my life. This was the start of my healing process because, for the first time, I had my answer regarding my daughter's father: let him go. No more confusion, no more feeling stuck, no more wondering when or if he was going to come back and be a part of his daughter's life. I believe when God tells you to do something, He also gives you the grace to do it. For the first time in a while, it was easy for me to let go of him.

# Breaking Soul Ties

Do you find yourself constantly thinking about your ex? Are you wondering when you will stop thinking about him and he becomes a distance memory? The answer is when you break the soul tie that was formed between the two of you. Soul ties are formed through a relationship with people. You can form good soul ties and bad or unhealthy soul ties. Each time that you have sex with someone other than your spouse, you are forming a soul tie with that person. Both of your souls are connected in the spirit realm, so what this means is that each person that he laid down with prior to sleeping with you, once you lay down and have sex with this man, you are now taking on his spirit and all the other spirits of all the other sexual partners he had in his past. Soul ties is what causes you to think about him when he's gone, feel like you still love him after he has repeatedly broken your heart and you just can't seem to get over him. In order for you to move on and stop thinking about him, you have to break the soul tie that was formed in the relationship.

Here are the steps to follow to breaking unhealthy soul ties from past relationships:

Step 1: On a sheet of paper, write down the names of the persons you have had a sexual relationship with.

Step 2: Adding to the list, write down the names of the people that you've formed an emotional connection but haven't had sex with.

Step 3: Say each name in prayer, asking God to break any unhealthy soul tie that was formed with or without your knowledge and to forgive you for entering into that relationship.

Step 4: Get rid of any items that are still reminding you of your ex that's around your house. (These items consist of teddy bears, lingerie, jewelry, clothes, shoes, wall décor, old love letters, songs, etc. ...)

Step 5: Go through your phone and delete all ex's phone numbers from your contact list.

Step 6: Go through your social media channels and unfriend all ex's from your Facebook page. Stop following your friends with benefits on Twitter. Block each one of them from all of your social media pages so that they cannot look you up and inbox you and you can no longer look at their page and see what's new in their life.

Step 7: Bless your home by walking into each area of your house and saying out loud, "Any evil spirits that were brought in here by \_\_\_\_, I command that you leave right now in Jesus name."

# Grieving the Breakup

In this chapter, I want to talk to you about the five stages of grief that you will experience after a breakup because if you don't understand what you are going through, you will start to think and feel as if you are going crazy when, actually, you are just grieving the breakup. You may go through a denial phase where you start lying to yourself, telling yourself that the two of you are on a break, he's just mad at you at the moment. He will come around eventually, but as the days goes by, nothing from him. He's not calling you and when you call him, your call goes straight to voicemail and each time, you get madder and madder.

The five stages of grief are denial, anger, bargaining, depression, and acceptance. In no particular order right after a breakup or any kind, you will go through this. There will be times when just the thought of hearing his name will make you mad, and everyone around you will start calling you mean because of all the anger you have towards your ex inside. There will also be times where you find yourself missing him, wanting to see him, and crying all the time, wondering what went wrong between the two; know that it is perfectly fine to experience this. You may also find yourself still holding on to hope that he will come around and be in his child's life. All of these emotions are perfectly fine to feel and go through. This is the grieving process that you have to go through in order to grieve the relationship and get him out of your system. This is why I don't recommend you jumping into another relationship because you still have wounds and unanswered questions going on inside of you that you need answers to. Since we're talking about closure, this is the thing: sometimes, the closure you are seeking to get from your ex, you can get just by watching his action. If you're wondering if he loved you, then find the answer in his action because when you know the true meaning of love, you will discover that love does not run out on you. Love does not turn its back on its child. What the two of you had was lust that ended when you got pregnant. If it were real love, he would have stayed and found a way to work things out with you and the child even if that means the two of you not being together. If you're wondering, *How he could turn his back on my child, but be there for the other children he had from the previous relationship;* if the father of your child never saw or met the child he had with you, then this is why it is easy for him to just walk away from his child because he has no attachment to your child. He has no bond with the child or no love for the child; in his eyes, that's your baby you chose to have. The other children he has by the other woman—he knows these kids; he already formed a bond, connection, love with the other children, which is why he's taking care of them and is in their life. I know it sounds harsh, but how can you love something or someone you never met? You can't, so this is why I say sometimes you have to give yourself closure by his action. For the mom whose child's father has met their child but is in and out of his child's life, then my advice to you is to look at his relationship with his own father. Was his father in his life? How is the relationship now that he is grown? Your child's father may have a fear inside of him that he is going to be just like his father, a deadbeat, not there, in and out of his life and so instead of facing it and proving his own thoughts wrong, he does what daddy taught him, which is to run from your responsibility. So while you're going through this grieving process, allow yourself to grieve the breakup, go through the process, feel the emotions and ask God to purge all the hurt and pain from your heart so that you heal from this situation.

# Forgive and Heal

Forgiving is for you, not him. Don't fall into the trap of thinking that if you forgive your child's father, then you are letting him off the hook and he will get away with what he did to you. Vengeance is mine says the Lord; trust and believe that God sees everything that was done to you and He is going to discipline him in the way of his choosing. I remember being so mad at my daughter's father for him choosing to not be a part of my daughter's life that I kept saying to myself, after the DNA test results come back that he is the father, I'm going to go onto Facebook and inbox all three of his other children with the DNA proof, letting them know they have another sister out here in this world that their father is not telling them about. I was fed up, hurt and tired of being mistreated and so one day as I got into my vehicle to go pick up my son from school, I turned on the radio to listen to my pastor's radio show and soon as I turned to the channel, I heard my pastor say, "God does not want you to expose them!" WOW! That was God speaking directly to me through my pastor telling me not to expose my daughter's father. I was mad and even asked, "But why, God?" In my eyes, it wasn't right for him to go on living life like he doesn't have a newborn baby out here. I felt in my spirit that God wanted me to trust Him and let the anger I had toward my daughter's father go, and so I made the decision in my heart to forgive him, let it go, and trust that God was going to deal with him in His timing, not mine. You may not like your child's father for what he did to you, leaving you while you were pregnant, watching you struggle while he lives life like your child does not exist, but in order for God begin to work in your life and change the situation around for the better, you must forgive. From the time my daughter's father told me he wanted me to have an abortion all the way up until my daughter was three months old, I suffered from migraine headaches. I never had this problem before, and I couldn't figure out why all of a sudden, almost every month, I would experience severe migraine headaches out of nowhere that would last for a week at a time. I went to the emergency one day while driving with my children in the vehicle. I had to pull over and push the OnStar button for help because a migraine came on so fast to where my vision was getting blurry; I was feeling dizzy, and my head was pounding. Out of fear and because my three children were in the car with me, I pulled over until the ambulance arrived and took me to the hospital. While at the hospital, the doctor ran a test on me to try and figure out what was wrong with me but couldn't find anything wrong, so I was discharged with the instruction to make an appointment with my doctor to have my head scanned. To make a long story short, I stopped having migraine headaches when I forgave my daughter's father. I look at unforgiveness like a seed that was never meant to be inside of your body. Each time that you hold on to it and refuse to forgive and stay mad and angry at whoever did you wrong or mistreated you, you're watering the seed, and after so long of you watering the seed, it causes your body to be at dis-ease, and all of this diseases come upon your body. There was a season when my mother would pass out at work, and she didn't know why because she ate right, did exercise, took care of her body and was in shape. She kept going to the doctor, trying to figure out what was causing her to pass out and all I could think about is all the anger, the frustration, resentment, and bitterness she held inside towards her mother. Could this be the reason why you're passing out at work? It's a reason why God commands for us to forgive those who hurt us because God knows holding on to unforgiveness opens the door for the enemy to come into your life or body and attack it, so do yourself a favor today and forgive.

Let's start the forgiveness process:

On a sheet of paper write, I forgive you, (say the person's name), for (say what you forgive them for). For example: I forgive you, Derrick, for leaving me while I was pregnant and abandoning your child and not being there when I needed you the most. As you go through this process, let it all come out; don't hold anything back. If you feel like crying while you are going through this process, then cry, don't stop your tears from falling, but allow yourself to feel the pain release from your body. There is a powerful quote I saw online that said, "Avoidance is not healing." In order to heal, you must face it, deal with it, and then grow through it. After you forgive them, then forgive yourself. I love James Fortune's song "I forgive me." It is so powerful, and it is a reminder of how we need to forgive ourselves for mistakes we made in our past. Simply close your eyes and look up to heaven and say, "I forgive myself …," and let the words flow freely out of your mouth.

Chapter 8: Healing through faith

"For I, the Lord am your Healer," (Exodus 15:26 NIV.)

"So what brings you in here today?" I am tired! Tired of the daddy issues, tired of wondering why my mother doesn't like me, tired of attracting men who only want sex from me, tired of all the fake people around me that only want to be bothered with me when it benefits them. I'm just tired of everything and everyone, and I'm ready to get down to the bottom of these unresolved daddy issues so that I stop attracting men who just want sex. I want to be in a relationship. I want to learn how to set boundaries with the people in my life so that they can stop picking and choosing when they want to be bothered with me. I'm ready to get down to the bottom of things and do the work. There comes the point in time in your life when you just get tired of it all. I knew I settled for less in men and allowed them to make me their side chick, but even though I didn't like it, I allowed them to do it, and that's what I wanted to get down to the bottom of in counseling—why I was allowing this from men?

The beginning of that year while I was fasting, I cried out to the Lord to heal my heart, my pain, all of the wounds inside of me. I had no clue how He was going to do it; I put my faith in God that He heard my prayers and was going to heal me and I believe that was the day when my healing began. Healing is a process; it takes time to heal all of the wounds that I encountered since my childhood. I thought I was going to be in counseling for a long time, a year or so, but the amount of time you need in counseling is determined by your level of determination of getting the help that you need. My therapist used a test to score my level of depression and anxiety, and my numbers were in the severe stages, 34 points to be exact. That's considered severe depression and severe anxiety. Because of my determination, showing up and doing every homework assignment in as little as four sessions, my scores went down to below five. I was no longer depressed but healed and happy. So how did God heal me from depression?

1. "Your faith has healed you" (Mark 10:52 NIV). After I got tired of feeling sorry for myself, I made up in my mind that I was ready to stop the pity party and was ready for God to heal me so that I could move on with my life. One of my prayer requests I took to God while fasting was for him to heal me from all the hurt and pain I experienced from my ex's, my family and friends. I was tired of hurting and needed God to come in and do what I couldn't do, which was heal

me from the inside out. I've believed that God heard my prayers and was going to heal me in His timing.

2. "Faith by itself, if is not accompanied by action is dead" (James 2:17). You can have all the faith in the world, believing God to change your life, but if you don't put some action behind it, God cannot operate in it. I recognized that I couldn't heal myself, let alone see my own problems. There is a quote that says you can't solve a problem with the same mindset that created it. I needed someone else other than my family and friends to come into my life and see what I couldn't see and to shed some truth on my life. I come from a family that doesn't believe in going to counseling for help. If I told my family that I was depressed, they would tell me, "Nothing is wrong with you; all you need is a nap and time away from the kids." Everything will be OK tomorrow, but the truth of the matter was that even though I tried taking a nap, once I woke up, those same problems, the darkness, the heartache was all still there, waiting on me, so I turned to counseling for help.

3. "And the truth will set you free" (John 8:32). There were some hard truths that I had to face in counseling. I had to face and deal with being raped at the age of

14. I had to face the daddy issues and why my mother and I couldn't get along. I had to face the truth of why I settle for less in men. God cannot operate in darkness, so in order to expose the enemy in your life, you have to shed light on the areas where he has hidden himself at and expose him with the truth.

4. "He heals the brokenhearted and binds up their wounds" (Psalm 147:3). The word "binds" means to tie up; when your child falls and scrapes his knee, you clean it and then cover it with a band-aid so that it can begin to heal. This is how the Lord Jesus Christ operates in a believer's life. He allows us to fall and keep bumping our head repeatedly until we surrender to Him and allow Him to come into our life to heal us. Jesus comes in, sheds light and truth on the darkness in our life and begins to clean us up. Truth is what stops the pain. The more of God's word that you get inside of you, the more that it can work in your life. "For the word of God is living and active. Sharper than any double-edged sword, it penetrates even to dividing soul and spirit, joints and marrow; it judges the thoughts and attitudes of the heart. Nothing in all creation is hidden from God's sight. Everything is uncovered and laid bare before the eyes of him to

whom we must give account" (Hebrews 4:12-13). I used God's word to turn my rejection into acceptance. I went from feeling unloved to knowing that I am loved, and God loves me. Jesus is the great physician that we all need in our life.

Here is a prayer for you to pray over yourself to activate God's healing in your life:

Heavenly Father, The Lord Rapha my Healer, I ask that You be my healer today. Lord, I ask that You heal all my emotional wounds, the hurt and pain and the heartache that I've experienced from the people in my life and from the relationships that I entered into that have hurt me. Do as Your word says, in Psalm 51:10, "Create in me a clean heart, O God, and renew a right spirit within me." I ask that You heal all the painful thoughts that I've experience and heal all the memories of the things that happen to me, heal all the hurtful words that were spoken to me and I ask that You take all those memories away and not allow me to remember them no more. In the name of Jesus. Amen.

## Chapter 9: Healing from mother wounds

Will my mom and I ever get along? Why doesn't my mother like me? How can a mother be jealous of her own child/daughter? These are the thoughts that constantly race through my mind from time to time and played a big part with me falling into a depression. Just at the thought of thinking your own mother who gave birth to you not liking you will cause you to feel and think that something must be wrong with you, but that's not always the case. I was at the point in my life where I was sick and tired of getting into it with other females because of my own unhealthy relationship I had with my mother. I was tired of replaying the same ole messages in my head about my mother. I was tired of hearing from certain family members how my mother was jealous of me and how she didn't like me. I was at the point in my life where I was ready for God to heal and restore my relationship with my mother. I didn't care who didn't like who or what she did to me; I just wanted this hurt, pain, and this empty void that was in my heart to finally go away and have peace within me.

As I prayed and cried out to the Lord concerning my relationship with my mother, the Lord began to place onto my heart a few things concerning my mother, which later gave me an understanding of why we have the type of relationship that my mom and I have. As I took my eyes off my mother and started looking at her own relationship with her mother, I discovered that the same type of relationship she had with her mother she had with me. As I asked my aunts and uncles about my mother's childhood growing up, I learned that my mother didn't have a childhood, but was placed in situations as a child where she had to fight to protect herself. This explained the anger my mother had towards her mother. My grandmother is the type of grandmother that keeps her strife between all of her children; she does not encourage her children to get along with one another but to fight one another. This gave me insight into how my mother raised my brother and I. She didn't encourage us to fight one another, but she also didn't encourage us to look out for one another or to be close to one another. Taking a look at my grandmother and mother's relationship was the beginning of understanding that it wasn't that my mother didn't like me; she just was repeating the pattern or the type of relationship that she had with her own mother off onto me. Is it right? Not at all, but if you take a look at how you raise your children, you might find some similarities in how your parents raised you. As I continue to look at my family, I notice that in my family line was a generational curse of mothers not getting along with their daughters. I will talk more about how to break generational curses in the next section on deliverance. I made the decision to break this generational curse with my daughter and me because I believed in having a healthy relationship with my daughter.

When I was in counseling, I learned what love means, how it looks, and how it's shown. This new knowledge on love helped me recognize that the way in which my mother loved me was in an unhealthy manner. My mother's definition of love is fighting, arguing, name calling, buying you things as her way of apologizing, but never admitting to where she was wrong and control and manipulation. That's not love and once I discovered that, I was able to heal the little girl inside of me. As I searched the scriptures in the Bible on love, I've found that God is love and this is where love comes from. Love builds you up, not tear you down. Love is patient, kind, and long-suffering. Love forgives and does not constantly bring up your past mistakes. Love trusts, protects, and preserves. With this new knowledge of love, I'm now able to recognize that my mother's way of loving her children is unhealthy; she does not know the true meaning of love.

The one thing that stood out to me in my scripture search on love is that God is love and love comes from God. If the person who is currently hurting you does not know God, this is the reason for the hurt. "If you love me, keep my commands" (John 14:15). "Whoever says, 'I know him,' but does not do what he commands is a liar, and the truth is not in that person" (1 John 2:4 NIV). God commands his children to love one another, to do good to one another, to help one another, to bear with one another in the time of suffering, but yet, the people in your life are constantly hurting you, mistreating you, and not there when you need them most. Could it be that they do not know God? When you know God and know what His word says, how can you continue to mistreat the people that you say you love? This was the revelation I had concerning my mother. At the time of this writing, she does not know God, and her fruit is showing it. Now, with this new knowledge, can I just wipe my hands off my mother and be done with her? Not at all, but I can love and respect her from a distance. The Bible tells us to guard our heart, so, because I know she can hurt me, I have to rely on the Lord to teach me and show me how to interact with her, and sometimes, that may mean loving your parents from a distance and having boundaries in your life.

Sharing the story of my relationship with my mother in this book is not to make her look like a bad mother, no, we all make mistakes. I share my story because, in my lifetime, I have come across other women who had similar situations with their own mothers—confused, hurt, blaming themselves, thinking and believing that something must be wrong with them because their own mother does not like them or is jealous of them. This is not the case. When you take a look at your mother's relationship with her own mother, the things that happened to her in her childhood such as rape or molestation, you will find the answer to the real problem. A great book I recommend for you to read is *Will I Ever Be Enough? Healing the Daughters of Narcissistic Mothers* by Dr. Karyl McBride. This book helped me a lot on how to deal with a narcissistic mother, and it will help you too.

# Chapter 10: Reject Me No More!

How many times have you heard the saying that rejection is God's protection? Too many, right? But I'm here today to remind you that this saying is true and once you realize it, your life will begin to change for the better. Rejection is a wound problem and if left untreated and dealt with, will and can turn into self-rejection. When you're dealing with rejection, you have to go all the way back to the root and dig that seed up. Rejection for me started as far back to the age of 14. At the age of 14, I lost my virginity and was raped all at the same time by my then boyfriend. After my boyfriend left and went home, he called me and asked me if we could be sex partners instead of boyfriend and girlfriend. Talk about a blow to the gut. I was hurt, mad, angry, sad, confused about what he had just done to me and all I could do was tell him no and hung up the phone. A week later, I heard of him drowning in a swimming pool. I really didn't know how to feel after that, and so I didn't. I went on about my life as if nothing happened. Since I didn't properly deal with what happened to me, I grew believing that I was only good for sex; I felt ugly; I thought I was stupid, I only liked guys who didn't like me and then would get mad when they end up not choosing me to be in a relationship with. This is the result of what rejection can do in a person's life if you don't deal with the problem.

Avoidance is not healing; you have to make yourself remember all of the times that you felt rejected and go as far back as you possibly can remember so that you can find the root and dig it up. Once you find the root and deal with it, then you expose it to the truth. John 8:32 says, "… and the truth will set you free." If you believe that your body is only good for sex, then speak 1 Corinthians 6:19 over yourself by saying, "My body is the temple of the Holy Spirit." If you believe that there's no purpose for your life, declare Jeremiah 29:11, "For I know the plans I have for you says the Lord, plans to prosper you and not to harm you, plans to give you a hope and a future." Whatever lie you believe about yourself, write each one of them down and then take out your bible and replace it with what God says about you.

It's not rejection; it's redirection. Get this in your spirit. I believe some people come into your life for a reason, a season, and a lifetime. Some people come into our life to teach us things we might need to know later on down the line and other times, the devil sends people into your life to distract you and get you off track. Recognize those individuals who are a distraction in your life and stop entertaining them so that you can get back on track and focus. Your child's father who refuses to have anything to do with his child, let him go; he already served his purpose in your life, which is by giving you a beautiful child. Now let him go. Don't try and hold on to someone who doesn't want to be in your life. His rejection is God's way of telling you, "He's not the one." Sometimes, NO means NEXT. What your child's father won't do, another man will do. Trust and believe.

It's time that you get around people who celebrate you, who speak life into you. No more hanging around people who tolerate you and make you feel like they are doing you a favor of talking to you. No, change your circle, get around people who hold the same vision as you do. Hang around those individuals who are doing something with their life, who have goals and are working towards accomplishing those goals every day. You are the CEO of your life, and it's time that you promote, demote, and terminate some relationships in your life.

## Change of Environment

In order for me to properly heal, I had to move away from what was picking at my wound—my family. I kept sensing in my spirit that my time was up at my current location and I really did want to move, but as I kept looking at my income, I didn't believe that I really could afford to move to another location. I wasn't working at that time, was on a limited income depending on child support and social security to take care of my children and I, but one thing God taught me was when God says "Go," it's time to go because He knows if you stay in that same location, you have the ability to get destroyed there. I made up my mind and decided that if God is telling me to move, then He will make a way, and with that, I moved across town from everyone. It felt so good being away from everything, the drama, the people, no more headaches, a fresh start. I cut everyone off. I didn't let anyone know where we were staying right off back or give them my new number. I needed a break from it all. I wanted to enjoy my new place and my children. My kids were happy and loved our new place, and everything seemed to be working out fine for us.

A month into my new place, I begin to sense in my spirit that the Lord wanted me to move so that He could get me ready for my calling. It was right here in my new home that God taught me how to pray, led me to get baptize and dedicate my children back to the Lord. God taught me about deliverance. He gave me dreams of things to come to pass in my future and gave me favor with people. None of these things would have taken place in my life at my old location; this is why God was telling me to move so that He could get me to a place that's quiet, free of distraction—a place where I can hear Him speak and develop me.

# Chapter 11: I Am Loved!

Everything that I was taught about love growing up was a lie. I was raised believing that love hurts. I watched my mother fight with her sisters and mother and have a love-hate relationship. I quickly learned that love came with conditions with certain people in my life. When I'm giving you what you want, then you love me, but when I stop, the love is taken away from me, and now you don't want to be bothered by me. In my relationship with men, I thought it was love when he acted jealously and constantly cheated on me. I just knew he couldn't live without me each time we would break up to make up. All of this is a lie and the day this revelation came to me was when I sat down and took it upon myself to learn what love really means.

As I searched the scriptures for love, I discovered that love comes from God. God is love! When you think about who God is, He is loving, caring, gentle, patience, merciful, awesome, a gentleman, compassionate, a friend to the friendless, a Father to the fatherless, provider, peace, and so many other things. As I continued to learn about love, I discovered that love builds up (1 Corinthians 8:1), love is patient and kind (1 Corinthians 13:4). Love is selfless, not selfish. Love gives, not take. Love forgives and walks with you through trying times. Love will not watch you destroy your life, but instead, will pull you to the side and rebuke you and tell you the truth in love. Love has no conditions; it's unconditional.

Tony Gaskins has a quote that says, "Love did not hurt you. The person who did not know how to love you hurt you and you confused the two." How many times have you declared "I'm not loving again because it's too painful"? Listen, love didn't hurt you; the man you chose to love, who did not know love, hurt you. The opposite of love is hate. You are either operating from a space of love or hate. Hate is what causes a man to turn his back on his child. He doesn't hate you or the child but himself. This was what set me free when I understood what was going on within my children's fathers. I kept asking myself, *How he could do me like that if he loved me?* He never did. What we had together was lust that ran out. Love sticks around and perseveres through tough times, but lust has an expiration date. Lust expired the day I said I was pregnant. I know it sounds harsh, and you may not want to hear this or even face it, but the truth is the truth. How many times has God left you? None! Because He loves you. Even when you mess up, God is still there with His grace and mercy.

# Love Language

Dr. Gary Chapman has a book *The Five Love Languages* that I suggest you read to discover what your love language is and how to help others love you better, and you do the same. One of my love languages is quality time, and once I discovered what my love language was, I was able to identify exactly why I always felt like the people in my life didn't love me. The reason was that they weren't spending any time with me. My mother is not the type that would just come over to your house to sit and play with her grandchildren. My mother likes to buy people things, so each time my mother would buy me things and drop it off at my home, I would look at what she bought me and then look at her to see if she was going to stay and talk with me at home. But the minute she leaves, I would get mad and angry inside. She's looking at me like, *What's the problem? I just bought you a leather coat and bought all your kids clothes and shoes too, isn't that enough?* And I'm thinking, *No, I want you to sit down and spend some time with me.* We constantly bumped heads with one another over a little misunderstanding. We weren't speaking each other's love languages, and therefore no one felt loved or appreciated.

Each time that I sit down to read the Bible and God reveals something to me or even rebuke me, I feel loved by God. The way I look at it is, God loves me so much that He is taking out the time to not only spend time with me, but He's also teaching me and pointing things out to me that I need to work on in my own life. That's love!

The purpose for you learning what your love language is is for you to be able to convey that to your spouse, your family and friends so that they are aware of how you receive and feel loved. Now, don't be selfish; as they are learning your love language, find out what their love language is as well and begin to speak their languages so that everyone is feeling loved and appreciated by one another.

## An attitude of Love

Before going through this process, I was considered to be mean, judgmental, arrogant, held grudges; I criticized people a lot without even realizing what I was doing; I pointed out everyone's flaws and was very self-righteousness. Who wants to be around a person like this? Exactly and for this reason, God had to show me 'me' so that I could change for the better. With this new knowledge of what love is, where it comes from, and how it is expressed to others, I had a choice to either start walking in love or continuing on being the same ole Taquila and continue to go through life all by myself. I chose to do something different and walk in love. I began to treat others better than I wanted to be treated. That same family of mine that turned their back on me, I began to love on them by going around them, spending time with them, helping them when I saw a need instead of waiting on them to ask for help. I became a giver with my time, knowledge, and money. I'm still a work in process, but thank God I'm not what I used to be. Everything that you are getting into your life is a reflection of you and the energy that you are putting out there. I thought I was protecting myself by telling people how it is and breaking promises with others.

That caused people to not trust me and not want to be around me. I pointed out everyone's flaws around me and didn't care how they felt or took it, but when my daughter's father told me about my jacked up life and how my own life was a mess, I was hurt and wished he never spoke those words to me. See, God had to give me a taste of my own medicine so that I could feel how I was making other people feel so that I change. God wants to change you and do a new thing in you. Don't wait until He gives you a dose of your own medicine before you change. Decide to change now, and to help you get started, I suggest you get James MacDonald book *Lord, Change My Attitude Before It's Too Late* to start with changing your attitude.

# Part 3: The Revelation: Deliverance

## Chapter 12: Breaking Generational Curses

"Christ redeemed us from the curse of the law by becoming a curse for us, for it is written 'cursed is everyone who is hung on a tree'" (Galatians 3:13 NIV).

God began to place on my heart that there were some generational curses I needed to break, not only in my life but also in my children's life. Have you got to the point where you're just tired of struggling? Living paycheck to paycheck, barely getting by? You tithe every month, pay all of your bills on time every month, try to build up a saving and right when everything seems to be going right in your life, all it takes is for one thing to happen and everything is thrown off track. God began to reveal to me that the problem wasn't that I wasn't making enough money or something I was doing, no; the problem was the curse that has been in my family bloodline for years that's preventing me from living the abundant, prosperity life that God created for me to live. As I took a look at each member of my family, we all had one thing in common—we all held the belief that you have to work hard for money and struggle too. That is not God! That is the spirit of poverty that you are dealing with and this is one of the things that God revealed to me that was in my life which he wanted me to deal with. I come from a family where daughters don't get along with the mothers; siblings don't support one another; diseases such as diabetes, high blood pressure, cancer, migraine headaches just to name a few all exist in my family bloodline. These are all curses that I was born into, and God was calling me to deal with. Galatians 3:13 talks about how Christ redeemed us from the curse of the law by becoming a curse for us, so this lets me know that as believers, we are not supposed to struggle financially, barely getting by, living paycheck to paycheck. Our body was never designed to be at dis-ease. Jesus Christ took away all of our sickness and diseases on the cross. "My people are destroyed from a lack of knowledge" (Hosea 4:6). It's time to get educated on what Jesus Christ did for you on the cross because if you don't, the enemy will continue to defeat you and make your life a living hell—if you don't get up now and learn exactly what you are fighting against. There comes the point in your life where you just get tired of struggling, you get tired of being tired, and you say, "Enough, devil, I'm coming after you, and I'm going to take back everything that you have stolen from me!"

# Bind and Loose

In Matthew 18:18, it says that whatever you bind on earth will be bound in heaven and whatever you loose on earth will be loosed in heaven. To bind means to tie, make secure, to chain, restrain, put a stop to, to arrest, handcuff. You have legal authority to bind up any works of darkness in your life in the name of Jesus. To loose means to untie, to set free, divorce, unlock, disconnect, etc. We are given legal authority in the name of Jesus to loose ourselves from the results of sin.

Matthew 12:29 says, "How can anyone enter a strong man's house and carry off his possessions unless he first ties up the strong man?" A strong man is the ruling spirit over a group of demons in an individual or family's life, and it must be bound and broken in the name of Jesus. When you are dealing with strongholds in your life such as mothers and daughters not getting along, you must first bind up the spirit that is over that thing in the name of Jesus. Sometimes to break a stronghold will require you to fast. Fasting weakens the flesh, and demons hate it when you fast because it weakens them. In order to break the strongholds in your life, I suggest that you fast for however long God tells you to fast to break this stronghold on you and your family. Think about a strong man that's holding you, and no matter what you do, you just can't seem to shake him to loosen his grip on you but thank God for fasting and the name of Jesus. God wants to show you that some of the problems that you're having in your life are a spiritual thing, and in order to win, you must fight God's way.

## Chapter 13: Call Him Out!

"I have received the power of the Holy Spirit to lay hands on the sick and see them recover, to cast out demons, to speak with new tongues. I have power over all the power of the enemy and nothing shall by any means harm me" (Mark 16:17-18).

One day as I was listening to my pastor preach, he said something that gave me clarity on what I was experiencing in my life; he said something: "The same way that you received deliverance, you can fall right back in it. You have to fight for your deliverance." Even though I went to counseling and did all the homework assignments and fasted and prayed, there were times in my life that I would feel depressed all over again and would wonder if God really delivered me from depression like He said He did. God led me to pick up a copy of John Eckhardt's Deliverance and Spiritual Warfare Manual, which revealed to me exactly what the problem was in my life—Deliverance. God revealed to me that in counseling, fasting, and through my faith, all of that healed me, but I still needed deliverance from the spirit of depression, lust, rejection, addiction, fear, and a host of other demons.

"When an impure spirit comes out of a person, it goes through arid places seeking rest and does not find it. Then it says, 'I will return to the house I left.' <sup>25</sup> When it arrives, it finds the house swept clean and put in order. <sup>26</sup> Then it goes and takes seven other spirits more wicked than itself, and they go in and live there. And the final condition of that person is worse than the first" (Luke 11:24-26). Did you catch the last sentence, "… **and the final condition of that person is worse than the first"?** When demons enter a person's body, they link up together, and as you see from the verse seven, other spirits more wicked than itself are all working inside of one's body. Demons work in groups to torment your mind and cause you to feel like you are going crazy or losing your mind. This is how I felt with depression; I could not think; I felt hopeless; it always felt like something heavy was weighing me down, which it was—a demon. I was looking online at this blog post that talked about depression and demons, and the picture is what caught my attention because it had a picture of a demon sitting on top of a woman's head, weighing her down, and I said to myself, *This is exactly how I felt.* The demons that operate with the spirit of depression are sadness, loneliness, suicide, death, self-destruction, gloom, and self-pity. The ruling spirit, leader, or strong man over this group is depression. When commanding demons to come out, you want to command the ruling spirit to come out with its entire grouping. Sometimes, you can reverse this process by commanding each spirit to come out, working your way all the way up to its ruling spirit, depression, and then casting it out too.

Are demons real?

You may be wondering if demons are actually real and if so, I want to turn your attention to a couple of scriptures of where we see Jesus cast out demons and they're submitting to His authority.

"Just then a man in their synagogue who was possessed by an evil spirit cried out, 'What do you want with us, Jesus of Nazareth? Have you come to destroy us? I know who you are-the Holy One of God!' 'Be quiet!' said Jesus sternly. 'Come out of him!' The evil spirit shook the man violently and came out of him with a shriek" (Mark 1:23-26 NIV).

"While they were going out, a man who was demon-possessed and could not talk was brought to Jesus. And when the demon was driven out, the man who had been mute spoke," (Matthew 9:32-33).

"They went across the lakes to the region of the Gerasenes. When Jesus got out of the boat, a man with an evil spirit came from the tombs, to meet him. This man lived in the tombs, and no one could bind him anymore, not even with a chain. For he had often been chained hand and foot, but he tore the chains apart and broke the irons on his feet. No one was strong enough to subdue him. Night and day among the tombs and in the hills he would cry out and cut himself with stones. When he saw Jesus from a distance, he ran and fell on his knees in front of him. He shouted at the top of his voice, 'What do you want with me, Jesus, Son of the Most High God? Swear to God that you won't torture me!' For Jesus had said to him, 'Come out of this man, you evil spirit!' Then Jesus asked him, 'What is your name?' 'My name is legion,' he replied, 'for *we* are *many*.' And he begged Jesus again and again not to send them out of the area. A large herd of pigs was feeding on the nearby hillside. The demons begged Jesus, 'Send *us* among the pigs; allow *us* to go into them.' He gave them permission, and the evil spirits came out and went into the pigs," (Mark 5:1-13).

After reading these scriptures, I want to point out a few things that you may have overlooked. Demons, upon recognizing Jesus, ran to Him and begged Him not to destroy them. Demons submit to the name and presence of Jesus. Demons have names just like you and I. When you think about the purpose of a name, it is to identify someone. Demons are identified by their names but thank God that there is a name that is above all names and at the name of Jesus, every knee should bow, in heaven and on earth and under the earth (Philip 2:9-10). Use the name of Jesus to destroy demons. I encourage you to study the book of Matthew and Mark on how Jesus dealt with demons.

How to command demons to leave the person: (taken from John Eckhardt Deliverance and Spiritual Warfare Manual pg. 69-70)

1. Address the spirit by name, and if that is not known, address it by function. You will learn either the name or the function of the demon through discernment of the Holy Spirit, or the demon will tell you its name. You can also ask it its name as Jesus did when He cast out demons (Luke 8:30).

2. Repeatedly remind these spirits that your authority is given to you by Jesus Christ who is far above all rule and authority (Eph. 1:21).

3. Remind them of their fate in Revelation 20:10 and other places in Scripture (Job 30:3-8). Use the statement "The Lord Jesus Christ rebukes you" repeatedly as a battering ram.

4. It is helpful to harass the demons to confess that Jesus Christ is their Lord.

5. Ruler demons often can be badgered for more information. You badger by commanding the evil spirits to release information that is vital to the

deliverance. It is similar to interrogating enemy prisoners.

6. At times, you will command the ruler demon to go and then clean out the lesser demons under him, and if that does not work, reverse the tactics. Start with the lesser demon and work your way up. You can simply say, "I command all spirits operating under the ruler to come out, in the name of Jesus."

7. Bind and separate interfering spirits as God leads.

8. There is no need to shout at demons since the battle is not in the flesh but in the Spirit.

9. Use the phrase, "Come Out!"

10. Close all open doors through which the enemy could return with seven others more wicked (Matt.12:43-45), and pray for the person to be filled with the Holy Spirit to seal their deliverance. Close out by praying for angels to protect and guard the person, and cover them with the blood of Jesus.

When demons are cast out, they normally leave through the mouth. Common manifestations of demons leaving the body are coughing, belching, vomiting, spitting, yawning, etc. …

# Part 4: The Development

## Chapter 14: Spiritual Warfare

"For our struggle is not against flesh and blood, but against the rulers, against the authorities, against the powers of this dark world and against the spiritual forces of evil in the heavenly realms," (Ephesians 6:12 NIV).

There is a battle going on around you and in you. Satan is after your mind, seeking to keep you from discovering your God-given purpose; he is also after your peace, your finances, and your children. You may think that the problem is your baby daddy; *if he would just help out with his child, then things will be fine.* I'm here today to tell you that we battle not against flesh and blood; satan is behind the battle you're fighting with your child's father. The battle you are up against is not a battle you can see, but a spiritual battle that needs to be fought in the spiritual realms. In order to beat the devil and kick him out of your life, you first have to recognize where he has hidden himself at in your life so that he's no longer defeating you and you have to use the weapons that God already supplied you with in order to defeat satan and his workers.

# The Armor of God

In Ephesians 6:14-18, Paul shares with us the armor of God that we need to put on and use in order to defeat the devil in our life. I love the fact that God is showing us how to get ready for battle. It's time to stop fighting one another, your family and friends and start going after the devil who is really the cause of the strife, the arguments, the drama, etc.

…

It tells us what to clothe ourselves in for battle daily in order to defeat the devil. I want to point verse 11 of Ephesians chapter 6 which says, "Put on the full armor of God," and it reminds us again in verse 13 to put on the full armor of God so that when the day of evil comes, you may be able to stand your ground. If any piece of your armor is missing, you are opening the door for satan to enter in and attack you, so you have to make sure that you are putting on the full armor of God daily.

The first Armor of God to put on is the Belt of Truth, which is what you based your life on. Knowing and doing the truth will help you live a stable life, but knowing the truth and not doing it opens the door for sin and satan to enter. "Anyone, then, who knows the good he ought to do and doesn't do it sins.," (James 4:17 NIV). So when the married man approaches you, asking for your number, talking about he going through something with his wife or he's separated and they don't live in the same house, give him the truth by telling him, "Thank you, but no, thank you, I choose to not participate in adultery; have a good day." Every area of your life have to be based on truth; your sexual life must be based on truth, which is to not have sex before marriage. Your financial life must be based on truth by not allowing any debt to remain outstanding and to make sure that you are tithing every month. Your physical life must be based on truth by honoring your body and taking care of your temple. Your spiritual life must be based on truth too by not just knowing what the word says but by actually doing it. Putting on the belt of truth daily will strengthen you and allow you to live a stable life.

The second Armor of God to put on is The Breastplate of Righteousness, which represents right living. We put this armor on by seeking God and His righteousness. We choose each day to live right, to have a pure heart, and live according to how the bible says that we are to live. God's commands become our commands; His thoughts become our thoughts. We begin to pray, according to Psalm 51:10, "Create in me a pure heart, O God, and renew a steadfast spirit within me." Each day as we read the word, study it, and meditate on what the word of God says, we become more like Christ, and we choose each day to live right.

The third armor to put on is The Shoes of the Gospel of Peace. What are shoes used for? To walk in them. So, every day, you are to make it your goal to walk in peace with everyone that you come into contact with. Now, there are going to be those individuals whom you just can't seem to please; it will seem like no matter what you do, they still have a problem with something, and that's OK. Your job is to be at peace with knowing that no matter what you do, they are always going to find something wrong. There are three people that you want to aim to be at peace with on a daily basis—peace with everyone else, yourself, and God. Having peace with yourself also means being content with what you already have in your life. When you worry and allow yourself to get upset or discontented with what you think you don't have, then now you're opening the door for satan to enter into your life. This will cause you to feel down, to look at what everyone else has and what you don't, and before you know it, your spirit is not at peace. Psalm 34:14 encourages you to seek peace and pursue it. Proverbs 14:30 says a heart at peace gives life to the body. John 14:27 says, "Peace I leave with you; my peace I give you. I do not give to you as the world gives. Do not let your hearts be troubled and do not be afraid." As you can see, peace is something that we already have deposited on the inside of us; we just have to choose to use peace when we come across that person that we really don't like. I like to say, call your peace home; declare out of your mouth when all hell is breaking loose in your life, "Peace be still," and it will. God is not looking for you to be perfect, but to live at peace with yourself, with Him, and with everyone else.

The fourth armor to put on is for you to take up the Shield of Faith. When you think about holding up a shield, what you're initially doing is holding it up to block whatever it is that's coming your way. Let's continue reading the rest of this verse, Ephesians 6:16. In addition to all of this, take up the shield of faith with which you can extinguish all the flaming arrows of the evil one. When you are extinguishing a fire, you are putting it out. Your enemy, satan, is going to come at you from all angles, simply because you are reading this book and you have to be ready and on guard for whatever he throws your way. I remember right after counseling, I was feeling good about myself, my future seemed hopeful and, plus, God told me that He was going to deliver me from depression. I remember a couple of days later, not having a good day and feeling a little down, the thought came to me, *God didn't really deliver you from depression; look at you again, feeling the same old way as before.* And you know what, I started to believe it for a second, but the devil is a liar; he is the father of lies, and there is no truth in him. I began to speak back to the devil and let him know that God will do exactly as He stated and that I am delivered from depression, and before I knew it, I kicked him out of my thoughts. This is a prime example of how satan will try and creep back into your life by causing you to doubt what God told you. He also uses discouragement to get you off track by telling you things such as your life is a mess, you're never going to get any better, you might as well stop with all that personal development stuff. He will also use difficulty to trick you and make you feel like God has forgotten about you and that God is the reason why things are so hard in your life. Listen, the devil is a liar, and he has only one purpose for you, which is to steal, kill, and destroy you, your hopes, and dreams. Defeat him at his onset by taking up your shield of faith.

The fifth armor to put on is The Helmet of Salvation, which protects your mind. The Bible tells us that we are to renew our mind with the word of God; this is what keeps the negative thoughts out of our mind by constantly renewing it with God's word. Philippians 4:8 tells us to think about whatever is true, whatever is noble, whatever is right, whatever is pure, whatever is lovely, whatever is admirable, if anything is excellent or praiseworthy, think about such things. God is giving us the tools on how to protect our mind from satan; we just have to do what the word says. When you're battling a depression, there will be times when you feel like you are losing your mind; that is the devil playing tricks on your mind. Don't give in to him; check your thoughts by paying attention to what you are thinking about and if it's negative or sad, then stop thinking about such thing and shift your thinking onto something else.

The sixth armor is the sword of the Spirit, which is the word of God. The sword of the spirit is when you're going after rather him coming after you. The way that you use this weapon is by knowing what the word says, memorizing scriptures, and knowing how to use scriptures strategically to defeat satan. Whatever you are going through at this moment, find a scripture to stand on and memorize it to heart so that when satan comes and whispers in your ear, you're going to always be alone, you say back to him, "Never will my God leave me nor forsake me, God is always by my side." When you feel like there is no purpose for your life, quote what the scriptures says, in Jeremiah 29:11, "For my God knows the plans He has for me, plans to prosper me and not to harm me, plans to give me something to hope for in my future." When satan reminds you that you're unlovable, even your parents don't love you, pull out Psalm 27:10, which says, "Though my father and mother forsake me, the Lord will receive me." Remind the devil that, according to Colossians 3:12, you are dearly loved by God. This is how you fight and defeat the devil. Don't just memorize any verse, but strategically memorize the verses that help you defeat the devil with. When scriptures are stored up in your mind, that is your sword, and each time satan tells you a lie, cut it with the word of God.

The last armor to put on daily is prayer. Did you see the movie "War Room"? Prayer is a weapon in itself used to defeat the enemy. In order to pray effectively, you must know what the word of God says and pray the word over your life daily. God taught me how to pray right here in my home. He started with teaching me how to memorize scriptures and speaking them out loud over myself, and as I would begin to pray, the Holy Spirit would bring back to my mind scriptures to pray over myself. He was teaching me how to be strategic in prayer and beat the enemy using the word of God.

## Chapter 15: Trust and Faith in God

"And this same God who takes care of me will supply all your needs from his glorious riches, which have been given to us in Christ Jesus" (Philippians 4:19 NIV).

What do you do when you're trying to work but can't afford childcare? You trust God! Right after having my daughter in 2015, I started panicking, thinking of how to take care of the kids. I'm the type of person that don't like to rely on child support, the state, or social security to take care of my children and me because it's not guaranteed; it can stop any day, and I'm out on the streets. I've been homeless before when it was just my son and I, but now I have three children, and I can't afford for us to be homeless again, so I have to get up and get a job. Each time that I would get hired at a job, I couldn't keep the job because of either the babysitter quitting on me, not being able to afford daycare, or getting laid off. Since having my daughter, I've had four jobs, all lasting for one month. The last job I worked at laid me off after working it for one month, and that's when it hit me that God wanted me home with my children, not working. I surrendered my will and stopped looking for jobs to work at because I knew what the end results were going to be and so I decided to stay at home with my children.

I thought God just wanted me at home with my children, but that's wasn't all; God also wanted to teach me how to live on a budget and to trust Him. I was on a very limited budget and after tithing, paying rent, light, and gas, I only had $95 to live on for the entire month. Now here is the crazy part: when I was working making more money than I had now, I was always late paying my rent and couldn't afford to tithe a dollar. Now that I'm living on a budget, my rent is paid on time every month, and I'm tithing too. It's funny how God does things and teaches us things.

# Get Your House in Order

While at home with my children, another thing God began to reveal to me was that He wanted me to get my house in order. What does this mean? For me, this meant many things such as get organized and clean out the clutter, get a handle on my kids, stop allowing the TV and the internet to raise them, and get everyone in my household back in right standing with God. My son at the time was having a lot of things going on with him while he would sleep at night. He was three years old, and each time that he went to sleep, he would wake up 45 minutes later, screaming and crying. At nighttime, it got worse to the point where he would wake up screaming, running away from something and sometimes not even recognizing me when I would try and wake him up from screaming and hollering. I took him to the doctor several times, only to be told that it's night terror and as he gets older, he will grow out of it. My mother intuition was telling me that it's something more than night terror that was going on within my son and I was going to figure it out. I took him to have a sleep test done for sleep apnea, and it was confirmed that once every hour, my son would stop breathing in his sleep. The doctors told me that his sleep apnea could be the reason why he's waking up, screaming and hollering. Something inside of me still believed it was something else that was causing him to experience restless night. One night as my son was sleeping, I was lying in bed awake, looking at him as he slept peacefully and then he started crying in his sleep; he then opened his eyes and looked toward the window and got up and started running away like something was coming after him. I called his name, and he ran into my arms, looking back in the direction of the window, and he began to calm down. I said to him, "Did you see something?" He shook his head yes, "Where was it?" I asked him, and he pointed over to the window, and at that moment, I knew that my son was being tormented in his sleep by evil spirits.

Why were evil spirits tormenting him in his sleep? The Lord began to reveal to me that my son had no covering and that he was open for satan's attacks. When God said "covering," I knew He was advising me to dedicate my children back to the Lord so that they could be up under His covering. I've made an appointment at my church to have my two children participate in the baby dedication, and one of the requirements before going forward was to meet with one of the pastors of the church. As I met with one of the pastors at my church, he explained the purpose of baby dedication and how the children are now under God's covering (confirmation). He asked me about my children and the relationship with their fathers, and I advise him that my oldest son's father is actively in my son's life; it's the other two fathers who are refusing to meet their children and be a part of their life. The words of the pastor to me next were: "God wants you to get in right standing with Him first, and then He will restore those relationships, and He's going to do it in a way that you will know it is God." With that, my children were dedicated to the Lord and in right standing with God.

There are two reasons why I shared the story of my son and the night terrors and dedicating my children back to the Lord. I shared the story of my son, according to doctors, experiencing night terrors to tell you, mom, to trust your instinct. Sometimes, doctors can be wrong and if God is placing it on your spirit that it's something else going on other than what the doctors advise you, continue to investigate until God reveals what's going on with your child. I believe that I was only able to sense God's prompting in my spirit because I am in tune with my spirit; I know how God speaks to me and when something is off in my life. You have to get in tune with your spirit and know how to hear God when He is speaking to you. God is peace, so when my peace is disturbed, and it just doesn't sit right in my spirit, I know that's God getting my attention about something.

The story of the baby dedication was to let you know that God is a God of order. Before dedicating my children back to the Lord, I was praying and asking God to restore the relationships with my children's fathers back to them, but how could He if my children are not in right standing with God? How could he restore someone who is not in right standing with Him first? I believe God heard my prayers, but before He could move and answer my prayers, I had to get my children right with God. If you are praying and asking God to restore the relationship with your children and their father, then first look at yourself and your children and make sure that you all are in right standing with God. Have you accepted the Lord Jesus Christ to be your Lord and Savior? If not, accept Him into your life now by repeating after me: Heavenly Father, I repent of my sins. I ask that You come into my life and be my Lord and Savior in Jesus name. Amen. Get your children dedicated back to the Lord and make it your goal to start living for the Lord from this day forward.

## Chapter 16: A New Identity

"Unless you know who you are, you will always be vulnerable to what people say." —Dr. Phil McCraw

I was told by my family that I was just like my mother, and when I get older, I was going to have ten kids too just like my aunt. Certain friends told me that I was mean and crazy. All of these things that were spoken over me was a lie from the pit of hell, and it was time that God sat me down and revealed to me who I am in Christ.

After doing my own research on the scriptures and learning who God says that I am, I discovered that God loves me, accepts me, chose me to be holy and blameless. I have the mind of Christ. I have the same attitude of Christ Jesus. I have the peace of God that passes all understanding. I have the power of the Holy Spirit to lay hands on the sick and see them recover, to cast out demons, to speak with new tongues. I have the power over all the power of the enemy, and nothing shall by any means harm me. Philippians 4:19 says that I have no lack for my God supplies all of my need, so I no longer have to wonder how I'm going to get by because God already stated that He is the one who supplies all of my needs. According to 1 Peter 2:9, God has called me out of darkness and into His marvelous light.

I am God's child, according to 1 Peter 1:23, and I am a new creation in Christ; the old has gone, the new has come, so I no longer have to act like my old self—cursing and fighting. The old Taquila is gone, and I am now a new creation in Christ. God also said that I am part of a chosen generation, so I don't have to fight to fit in with certain people; I'm already chosen. It also says that I'm a royal priesthood, which means, I'm valuable, a holy nation, a purchased people, a people belonging to God (1 Peter 2:9). Colossians 3:12 says that I am God's daughter, holy and dearly loved, full of compassion, kindness, humility, gentleness and patience. Now, I can stop believing the lies my family spoke over me, saying that I'm mean and crazy. I can go on and on about who I am in Christ, but in order for you to overcome depression, you must learn who you are in Christ. One of the reasons why you are feeling depressed is because you believe the lies of the enemy that you're unworthy, people don't like you, there is no hope for you—all of this is lies from the pit of hell.

Satan is the father of lies, and he will do whatever he can to keep you from learning the truth about who you are in Christ. You must become aware of satan's schemes and tactics that he uses in your life. He will cause your parents to reject you and tell you lies such as you are stupid; you will never be anything; you are just like your father or mother. He will use relationships close to you, people that you look up to and respect to hurt you and speak lies over you, which is why you must learn the truth of who you are in Christ on your own. Don't take my word for it; study the scriptures for yourself, learn the word, and see what it says regarding who you are for yourself so that you're able to defeat the enemy when he whispers, "Don't nobody love you," and you say back to him, "I am greatly loved by God." The way in which you can defeat the devil is by speaking the word, the bible, scriptures back to him to remind him that Jesus Christ defeated him on the cross and that he has to get behind you.

**Who else does God say that I am in Christ?**

**God says …**

I am forgiven (Ephesians 1:7).

I am fully capable (1 Peter 2:9-10).

I am chosen (1 Peter 2:9).

I am extremely valuable, priceless, and holy (1 Peter 2:9-10).

I am the head and not the tail; above all and not beneath (Deuteronomy 28:13).

I am complete in Him (Colossians 2:10).

I have the mind of Christ (1 Corinthians 2:16).

I have the peace of God that passes all understanding (Philippians 4:7).

I can do all things through Christ who strengthens me (Philippians 4:13).

I am a new creature in Christ (2 Corinthians 5:17).

I am more than a conqueror through Him that loves me (Romans 8:37).

I am the light of the world (Matthew 5:14).
By his wounds, I have been healed (1 Peter 2:24).

I am called of God to be the voice of His praise (Psalm 66:8).

I am loved by God (Romans 1:7).

I do not fear because God has given me power, love, and a sound mind (2 Timothy 1:7).

I am God's workmanship (Ephesians 2:10).

I am redeemed from the curse of sin, sickness, and poverty (Galatians 3:13).

I am firmly rooted, built up, established in my faith, and overflowing with gratitude (Colossians 2:7).

I am God's daughter, holy and dearly loved, full of compassion, kindness, humility, gentleness, and patience (Colossians 3:12).

This is who you are; this is your identity in Christ. Get rid of the old identity and start walking in your new identity today.

## Chapter 17: A New Family

When God placed on my heart to relocate and move away from my family, I did exactly as he advise me to do. But because I was living across town from my family, there were days where I found myself missing being around my family, missing all the kids coming to my house to play with my children, and I started to feel all alone again. One night as I laid down in bed to go to sleep, God gave me a dream of a faceless person splashing water on me. In the dream, it felt like the faceless person was cleansing me … but of what?

Two months after having the dream of the faceless person splashing me with water, I was sitting in my baptism class, and I heard the teacher say that when you get baptized, the Lord God is cleansing you. Immediately after hearing those words, I thought about the dream I had two months ago; the Lord was guiding me to get re-baptized again so that He could cleanse me. In one of my pastor sermons, he talked about how when you get baptized, the Holy Spirit comes upon you and gives you the power to do God's will for your life.

Shortly after getting baptized, I still had my days of feeling down, all alone, and even depressed. I decided to start attending our women of purpose connection group on Thursday nights just to be around other like-minded women, and I'm so happy and thankful that I did. We were all assigned different tables to sit at, and each table had a leader/minister assigned at the table to keep things flowing. At my table was a lady named Minister Fuller that I'm so grateful that the Lord allowed me to meet and get to know. Each week as I attended the class and participated in the activities, I began to reveal to the people at my table my battle with depression and being a single mom. To my surprise, I got no judgment but love from them. Minister Fuller made it her business to keep in touch with me after the class was over just to check and see how I was doing and that made me feel good inside. She would pray for me when God placed me on her heart to pray for, and even though she didn't know why I was on her mind, she prayed for me anyway.

In a short period of time, people from my church would pick up the phone and call to check on me and my children and make sure we had everything we needed. My church made sure that even though I was a single mother raising three children by myself, they walked with me and let me know that I didn't have to go through this time in my life all by myself. They showed me how a family loves on one another and I'm forever thankful for them because it was their love that got me through many lonely nights and days. It was their love that kept me connected to the church, doing the right thing. It was their love and encouragement that pushed me not to give up. Because they believed in me, I believed in myself. They showed me God's love in action.

God showed me the importance of having a church home and getting and staying connected to them. No single mother should go through life all by herself because it opens the door up for satan to enter into your life and get inside of your mind, telling you thoughts such as "no one loves you, your life will always be like this, there's no hope for you, etc. ..." The devil is a liar, and there is hope for you. I highly recommend if you don't already have one, getting into a good bible based church where they not only teach the word but also live the word right in front of you. Ask God to guide you to the right church for you and He will because He did it with me. Before joining my church, I listened to my pastor for one whole year on the radio before even attempting to go to his church. I wanted to make sure that I understood exactly what he was saying and preaching and I did and was also learning a few things too, and so, after one year, I decided to visit his church but got lost in route to the church. I prayed and asked God to show me where the church was at before turning around and going home, and I felt in my spirit to turn right, and I did, and there was the church. That day, I gave my life back to the Lord and later joined the church. It can be as simple as that. Get connected to a good church home, let them know what's going on in your life, and receive the help that they are offering to you, but whatever you do, don't go at life alone; get connected.

# Chapter 18: Prayer

One day after church, I felt in my spirit that I should pray specially for my daughter and my second son's fathers and believe God to turn their hearts back to their children and give them the desire to want to meet their children and be a part of their life. I also began to sense in my spirit that I should ask one of my friends who was in a similar situation as I was concerning her son's father to come into agreement with me in prayer and so I did. To my surprise, she, too, stated that she was thinking about asking me to do the same thing with her, but wasn't sure how I would respond to it. That was my confirmation that what we both were sensing in our spirit was from the Lord—wanting us to come together and pray for our children's fathers. We decided to pray for seven days standing on God's word in Malachi 4:6 that says, "He will turn the hearts of the father back to their children and the children's hearts back to their fathers," and for the next seven days, we prayed like never before. I'm a firm believer that if you stand on God's word and repeat back to God what His word says, he will move in that situation. In the seven days of prayer, I noticed how I prayed. The Lord would bring certain things to mind to pray about concerning my children's fathers such as to soften the father's heart toward me, their mother, and allow them to forgive me for any hurt or pain that I might have brought to their lives, which I'm not even aware of. I asked God to place in my children's fathers a new heart and a right spirit and give them new eyes to see their children with. After the seven days was over, I had a dream that I was 6 months pregnant, and I woke up. I knew, from my previous study of different dream meaning, that when you dream of being pregnant, it means "bringing something forward or birthing something," and so I began to get excited as I called my friend up on the phone and told her about my dream and what it meant. A week later, after my pregnancy dream, while my friend was sitting in church, her pastor preached a sermon on being pregnant and birthing something. I knew when she called me and told me what her pastor preached that that was God confirming to both of us that He heard our prayers and in His timing, we were going to see the very thing that we prayed for happen.

I believe that the Lord used that moment to show me the power of prayer. Before that time, I had no prayer life; I would only pray when I found myself in certain situation that I really needed God to get me out of, but since that day and reading books on prayer and really getting an understanding of it and how to get your prayers answer by God, I loved praying. Priscilla Shirer has a book *Fervent Prayer* that I highly recommend you read because it was that book that helped me understand how to be strategic in your prayer and beat the devil at his tactics that he throws your way. I also recommend that if your child's father is not currently in his or her child's life and it's your heart desire for your child to know their father, then take your request to God in prayer. Stand on God's word in Malachi 4:6 and remind God of what His word says and ask Him for whatever it is that you are looking for Him to do in your child's father's life and believe that He is going to do it. It says, in Numbers 23:19 NIV, "God is not a man that he should lie"; repeat His word back to him and watch God move in your life.

## Chapter 19: Purpose and Calling

"For I know the plans I have for you, declares the Lord, plans to prosper you and not to harm you, plans to give you hope and a future" (Jeremiah 29:11 NIV).

God turned my mess into a message to bring hope to other single moms. In my pain, God birth my purpose. You never know how God is going to use you to influence the masses, but I am so thankful that He chose me to use my story to help others. God has given me a burden for single mothers. I know what you are going through. I understand the struggle, the pain, not knowing how to answer the question: "Mommy, where's daddy?" My purpose and calling in this season of my life is to bring awareness to the things that single mothers face in their own life. To be a voice for those feeling pressure to abort their unborn child, and to encourage you to choose life. I was asked the question, "When did I discover what my purpose was?" and the answer is simple when God told me my book title: "From Depression to Deliverance." Even though at that time I did not know how I was going to explain exactly how God delivered me from depression in a book format, but the urgency in my spirit was confirmation that God had a message that He wanted to birth out of me. The other confirmation of the message that God wanted me to share with other single moms came several times from one of my YouTube videos I made last year in 2016, entitled "He wants an abortion, but I don't." Out of all the videos on my YouTube channel, this video is one of the videos until this day that women are finding, watching, and leaving me comments on how what I said made them cry and made them change their mind of aborting their child. I have received so many emails from women who are currently pregnant and feeling pressure to abort by their boyfriend because he is threating to leave. This is one video God is using to impact and reach single mothers to encourage them to choose life. This is my purpose.

# How to Discover your Purpose

The definition of purpose is the reason for which something is done or created for which something exists. You were created with and for a purpose. Everything that you have experienced in your life is all leading and guiding you towards your God-given purpose. Whatever you have overcome in your life, God wants you to use it and share it with others so that they, too, have hope, knowing that they can beat and overcome whatever it is that they are facing in their own life. Don't keep it a secret. Do not allow the devil to cause you to feel ashamed of what you've been through or what has happened to you in your past. Use it to help the next woman. The day I heard Joyce Meyer speak about being raped by her father repeatedly was the day I begin to open up and talk about being raped by my own boyfriend at the age of 14. If she never told her story, I probably would have never told mine. There is power in sharing your story.

Most people say, "How do I find my purpose?" You don't find your purpose; you discover it day by day. God allowed you to be born for a specific purpose that He has in mind for you to fulfill. Listed below are some tips to help you discover your purpose.

1. Identify what your spiritual gifts are. The spiritual gifts that God equipped you with are going to help you to carry out your mission and assignment. Everyone has different spiritual gifts, but they're all used for the same purpose—to give God all the glory. My top three spiritual gifts are serving, mercy, and exhortation. I'm a server at heart. Wherever my help is needed, I'm there on time, ready to serve. I have the gift to make others feel comfortable with talking to me about their most pressing problems and not feel judged. I also have the gift to inspire hope and encouragement. I encourage you to find out what your spiritual gifts are by taking the assessment test at www.churchgrowth.org.

2. What has God given you a burden for? What is it that God has placed in your heart to do that won't go away? I always knew that I was called to build and encourage women. People told me all the time that I gave great advices and I was very encouraging after listening to me speak. Whatever it is that you feel in your heart that God is prompting you to do, then get busy doing it. Don't worry about the how; just do what you can with what you already have right now.

3. What have you been through and have overcome in your own life? This could be connected to your calling. A few people that I want to highlight here in my hometown Detroit, Michigan that are using their own story to change lives are Dr. Eddie Conner who is a survivor of stage four cancer and empowers people to overcome obstacles. My book coach, Kim Brooks, is sharing her own personal story of being a virgin and encouraging other Christian singles and how to be single, saved, and celibate until marriage. Your story is connected to your purpose.

4. What has God told you to do? Many times when God tells us or reveals to us what our purpose is, we tend to fight it. For whatever reason, we get afraid and feel like we don't have what it takes to do this particular thing that God is telling you to do. Know that whatever God is telling you to do, you already have what you need in you to do it. Trust God and don't fight what He is telling you to do.

5. Pray and ask God to give you a clear vision of your purpose. Now, do not get discouraged if God does not reveal your purpose right away to you because you may not be ready to handle all of what He is calling you to do. Have faith in knowing that God's word is

true, just like He said in Jeremiah 29:11, "For I know the plans for your life says the Lord, plans to prosper you and not to harm you." God knows your purpose, the plan He has for your life, so trust in His timing of revealing your purpose to you.

Some books I recommend you start reading regarding purpose is *The Purpose Driven Life* (by Pastor Rick Warren), *Kingdom Dreaming* (by my pastor Christopher Brooks,) and *Destiny* (by Bishop T. D. Jakes). Read these books to help you step into your purpose.

Lastly, in closing, I would like to invite you to be a part of our single moms' group over on Facebook. I believe in no mother going through life all alone with no support. God created us to be in a relationship with one another. Come and be a part of a group of women who support, encourage, and lift one another up over in our Facebook group called "Single Mothers Raising Children without Fathers." Join us; we love to welcome you to our community. You can also find us on meetup.com if you live in Michigan and are looking to connect with like-minded individuals and build lasting relationships. Feel free to reach out to me at www.TaquilaColeman.com and connect with me on all social media channels @TaquilaColeman

# Scriptures on Love (NIV)

You love righteousness and hate wickedness (Psalm 45:7).

Praise be to God, who has not rejected my prayer or withheld his love from me (Psalm 66:20)!

For great is your love toward me (Psalm 86:13).

To proclaim your love in the morning (Psalm 92:2).

When I said, "My foot is slipping," your love, O Lord, supported me (Psalm 94:18).

**For the Lord is good and his love endures forever (Psalm 100:5).**

Crowns you with love and compassion (Psalm 103:4).

So great is his love for those who fear him (Psalm 103:11).

I love the Lord, for he heard my voice; he heard my cry for mercy (Psalm 116:1).

Give thanks to the Lord, for he is good, his love endures forever (Psalm 118:1).

The earth is filled with your love (Psalm 119:64).

May your unfailing love be my comfort (Psalm 119:76).

For with the Lord is unfailing love (Psalm 130:7).

The Lord is gracious and compassionate, slow to anger and rich in love (Psalm 145:8).

Let love and faithfulness never leave you, bind them around your neck, write them on the tablet of your heart (Proverbs 3:3).

I love those who love me, and those who seek me find me (Proverbs 8:17).

Love covers over all wrongs (Proverbs 10:12).

**Surely it was for my benefit that I suffered such anguish. In your love you kept me from the pit of destruction; you have put all my sins behind your back (Isaiah 38:17).**

For I the Lord, love justice (Isaiah 61:8).

In his love and mercy he redeemed them (Isaiah 63:9).

Who keeps his covenant of love with all who love him and obey his commands (Daniel 9:4).

For he is gracious and compassionate, slow to anger and abounding in love (Joel 2:13).

The Lord your God is with you, he is mighty to save. He will take great delight in you, he will quiet you with his love (Zephaniah 3:17).

Love truth and peace (Zechariah 8:19).

This is my son, whom I love, with him I am well pleased (Matthew 3:17).

Love your enemies (Matthew 5:44).

Love your neighbor as yourself (Matthew 19:19).

Love one another as I have loved you, so you must love one another (John 13:34).

If you love me, you will obey what I command (John 14:15).

God has poured out his love into our hearts by the Holy Spirit, whom he has given us (Romans 5:5).

**But God demonstrates his own love for us in this: While we were still sinners, Christ died for us (Romans 5:8).**

And we know that in all things God works for the good of those who love him (Romans 8:28).

**Love must be sincere (Romans 12:9).**

**Love does no harm to its neighbor (Romans 13:10).**

## Love builds up (1 Corinthians 8:1).

Love is patient, love is kind. It does not envy, it does not boast, it is not proud (1 Corinthians 13:4).

**Love does not delight in evil but rejoices with the truth (1 Corinthians 13:6).**

Love never fails (1 Corinthians 13:8).

Serve one another in love (Galatians 5:13).

Being rooted and established in love (Ephesians 3:17).

Be completely humble and gentle; be patient, bearing with one another in love (Ephesians 4:2).

**Speaking the truth in love (Ephesians 4:15).**

May the Lord direct your hearts into God's love and Christ perseverance (2 Thessalonians 3:5).

Above all, love each other deeply, because love covers over a multitude of sins (1 Peter 4:8).

But if anyone obeys his word, God's love is truly made complete in him (1 John 2:5).

How great is the love the Father has lavished on us, that we should be called children of God (1 John 3:1).

**Let us love one another, for love comes from God (1 John 4:7).**

And so we know and rely on the love God has for us (1 John 4:16).

**We love because he first loved us (1 John 4:19).**

**Those whom I love I rebuke and discipline (Revelation 3:19).**

Who keeps his covenant of love with those who love him and obey his commands (Nehemiah 1:5).

# Scriptures on Healings

He heals the brokenhearted and binds up their wounds (Psalm 147: 3 NIV).

"My son, pay attention to what I say; listen closely to my words. Do not let them out of your sight, keep them within your heart; for they are life to those who finds them and health to a man's whole body" (Proverbs 4: 20-22 NIV).

"O Lord my God, I called to you for help and you healed me" (Psalm 30:2 NIV).

"The Lord will protect him and preserve his life; he will bless him in the land and not surrender him to the desire of his foes. The Lord will sustain him on his sickbed and restore him from his bed of illness" (Psalm 41: 2-3 NIV).

"Praise the Lord, O my soul, and forget not all his benefits-who forgives all your sins and heals all your diseases, who redeems your life from the pit and crowns you with love and compassion" (Psalm 103:2-4 NIV).

"He said to her, "Daughter, your faith has healed you. Go in peace and be freed from your suffering" (Mark 5:34 NIV).

"He himself bore our sins in his body on the tree, so that we might die to sins and live for righteousness; by his wounds you have been healed" (1 Peter 2:24 NIV).

"Worship the Lord your God, and his blessing will be on your food and water. I will take away sickness from among you" (Exodus 23:25 NIV).

# Scriptures on Identity

1. I am redeemed from the hand of the enemy (Psalm 107:2).
2. I am forgiven (Colossians 1:13, 14).
3. I am saved by Grace through Faith (Ephesians 2:8).
4. I am Justified (Romans 5:1).
5. I am Sanctified (1 Corinthians 6:11).
6. I am a New Creature (2 Corinthians 5:17).
7. I am Delivered from the Powers of Darkness (Colossians 1:13).
8. I am led by the Spirit of God (Romans 8:14).
9. I am Free from all bondage (John 8:36).
10. I am kept in Safety wherever I go (Psalm 91:11).
11. I am strong in the Lord and in the Power of His Might (Ephesians 6:10).
12. I am doing all things through Christ who strengthens me (Philippians 4:13).
13. I am an Heir of God and a Joint Heir with Jesus (Romans 8:17).
14. I am heir to the blessings of Abraham (Galatians 3:13, 14).
15. I am blessed coming in and blessed going out (Deuteronomy 28:6).
16. I am an heir of Eternal Life (1 John 5:11, 12).

17. I am blessed with all spiritual blessings (Ephesians 1:3).

18. I am healed by His stripes (1 Peter 2:24).

19. I am above only and not beneath (Deuteronomy 28:13).

20. I am more than a conqueror (Romans 8:37).

21. I am an overcomer by the blood of the lamb and the word of my testimony (Revelation 12:11).

22. I am walking by Faith and not by sight (2 Corinthians 5:7).

23. I am casting down vain imaginations (2 Corinthians 10:4, 5).

24. I am bringing every thought into captivity (2 Corinthians 10:5).

25. I am being transformed by renewing my mind (Romans 12:1-2).

26. I am the righteousness of God in Christ (2 Corinthians 5:21).

27. I am an imitator of Jesus (Ephesians 5:1).

28. I am the light of the world (Matthew 5:14).

29. I am alive with Christ (Ephesians 2:5).

30. I am set free of the law of sin and death through Christ Jesus (Romans 8:2).

31. I am far from oppression and fear does not come near me (Isaiah 54:14).

32. I am born of God, and the evil one does not touch me (1 John 5:18).

33. I am chosen in him before the creation of the world to be holy and blameless in his sight (Ephesians 1:4).

34. I am holy because He is holy (1 Peter 1:16).

35. I have the peace of God that passes all understanding (Philippians 2:5).

36. I have received the gift of righteousness and reign (rule) as a king in life by Jesus Christ (Romans 5:17).

37. I have received the spirit of wisdom and revelation in the knowledge of Jesus, the eyes of my understanding being enlightened (Ephesians 1:17-18).

38. I have received the power of the Holy Spirit to lay hands on the sick and see them recover, to cast out demons, to speak with new tongues. I have power over all the power of the enemy, and nothing shall by any means harm me (Mark 16:17-18).

39. I have put off the old man and have put on the new man, which is renewed in the knowledge after the image of Him who created me (Colossians 3:9-10).

40. I have given, and it is given to me; good measure, pressed down, shaken together, and running over, will be poured into your lap (Luke 6:38).

41. I have no lack for my God supplies all of my needs according to His riches in glory by Christ Jesus (Philippians 4:19).

42. I can quench all the fiery darts of the wicked one with my shield of faith (Ephesians 6:16).

43. I show forth the praises of God who has called me out of darkness into His marvelous light (1 Peter 2:9).

44. I am God's child for I am born again of the incorruptible seed of the word of God, which lives and abides forever (1 Peter 1:23).

45. I am God's workmanship, created in Christ Jesus to do good works, which God prepared in advance for us to do (Ephesians 2:10).

46. I am a new creation in Christ; the old has gone, the new has come (2 Corinthians 5:17).

47. I am a spirit being alive to God (1 Thessalonians 5:23).

48. I am a believer, and the light of the Gospel shines in my mind (2 Corinthians 4:4).

49. I am a doer of the Word and blessed in my actions (James 1:22, 25).

50. I am a joint-heir with Christ (Romans 8:17).

51. I am a partaker of His divine nature (2 Peter 1:3-4).

52. I am an ambassador for Christ (2 Corinthians 5:20).

53. I am part of a chosen generation, a royal priesthood, a holy nation, a purchased people, a people belonging to God (1 Peter 2:9).

54. My body is a temple of the Holy Spirit, who is in me, whom I have received from God. I am not my own (1 Corinthians 6:19).

55. I will lend to many nations but will borrow from none. I am the head and not the tail. I am always at the top, never at the bottom (Deuteronomy 28:13).

56. I am the light of the world (Matthew 5:14).

57. I am God's daughter holy and dearly loved, full of compassion, kindness, humility, gentleness and patience (Colossians 3:12).

58. In him I have redemption through his blood, the forgiveness of sins (Ephesians 1:7).

59. For he has rescued me from the dominion of darkness and brought me into the kingdom of the Son he loves (Colossians 1:13).

60. I am redeemed from the curse of sin, sickness, and poverty (Galatians 3:13).

61. I am firmly rooted, built up, established in my faith and overflowing with gratitude (Colossians 2:7).

62. I am called of God to be the voice of His praise (Psalm 66:8).

63. By his wounds I have been healed (1 Peter 2:24).

64. And God raised me up with Christ and seated me, with him in the heavenly realms in Christ Jesus (Ephesians 2:6).

65. I am strengthened with all might according to His glorious power (Colossians 1:11).

66. I am submitted to God, and the devil flees from me because I resist him in the name of Jesus (James 4:7).

67. For God did not give me a spirit of fear, but a spirit of power, of love, and of self-discipline (2 Timothy 1:7).

68. It is not I who live, but Christ lives in me (Galatians 2:20).

# About Taquila Coleman

Taquila Coleman is an entrepreneur, motivational speaker, and personal life coach with a mission to heal and support women on a journey of self-discovery and confidence after divorce, abuse, or life-altering events. With a life mission of restoring the souls of women to allow them access to their fearless, authentic, whole selves, Taquila is equipped with a simple, no-nonsense approach that makes her inspiring, authoritative, and effective.

Taquila's journey began following the dissolution of her marriage when she recognized that she had lost herself and her identity in her husband. With renewed faith in God and determination to face the abuse and low self-esteem of her childhood, Taquila worked on herself before realizing her gift and life mission was to support women going through the same trauma that she herself had experienced. She became a Life Coach, obtained a Lay Counselor Certificate, and authored the book, The Confident Sista Hand Book.

Presently, Taquila provides customizable, highly personalized group and individual services to women who are searching for themselves in the rubble life has left in front of them. Taquila gives women hope, knowledge, and the tools to recreate their lives using the greatness that's already inside them. Truly honored to do this work, Taquila is grateful to instill her sense of pride, strength, and accomplishment in the women she encounters.

Proof

Made in the USA
Columbia, SC
03 October 2017